PENCOM INTERNATIONAL books are available at special discounts when purchased in bulk for premiums and sales promotions as well as for fundraising or educational use. Special editions can also be created to specification. For details contact PENCOM INTERNATIONAL at the address above. Thank you.

ISBN 1-879239-05-1
2 — 6/97

Our sincere thanks to all the restaurant owners, operators and managers who contributed their valuable ideas to this book, and to Natalie Hanlon-Leh for her legal expertise.

Graphics and design by Deborah Henckel.

TURN THE TABLES ON TURNOVER

52 Ways To Find, Hire and Keep
the Best Hospitality Employees

CONTENTS

"Lousy, incompetent, uninterested, sloppy, uncaring, clumsy, feeble, robotic, unfeeling, artless, careless, inept, unqualified, pretentious (pick your adjective) service is traceable to 'the whole service issue' and the lack of skilled help."

—Stephen Michaelides, Associate Publisher of the Penton Foodservice Group

IMPORTANT

This book is intended to inform you generally as to important aspects of recruiting, hiring and training employees. The information contained in this book is based upon the state of the law as of the date of publication, and the authors and publisher assume no responsibility to provide updates as relevant laws may change. In addition, its particular application to your operation may vary depending on the specific characteristics of your operations as well as relevant state law, which varies from state to state. You should consult with your own legal counsel regarding particular employment decisions and policies in your operation.

THE TURNOVER EPIDEMIC

If turnover isn't your restaurant's greatest ongoing challenge, you're either operating on another planet or you've employed the services of a robotics company to supply quality workers. Because every owner, operator and manager we've talked to has identified turnover as their number-one challenge — the one looming obstacle that prevents their otherwise successful business from getting ahead.

New restaurants are popping up at a rabbit's pace in this country: In the coming years, an average of 42 new restaurants will open *every day*. That's 294 a week or over 15,000 a year. Those new operations will not only have to compete for customers, they'll have to compete for employees. You think you have a turnover crisis now? Where will you be in a few more years? Combine that increasing competition with a younger generation's decreasing desire to launch their careers from the foodservice industry — and you've got yourself a turnover epidemic.

You don't need Nostradamus to tell you that a lot of those operations won't make it. But the number-one reason they'll fail *isn't* turnover. It's poor customer service. And that's what this book is all about. Because what some savvy operators already realize is that turnover has a profoundly negative effect on the service their guests receive.

Customers *hate* turnover. Why? Service becomes inconsistent or shuts down completely. Managers and staff are cranky from working double shifts. All the extra cost of continually recruiting and training new employees has to be covered somewhere — that could mean raising menu prices. And pity the poor customers who have questions about the menu, for they'll most likely hear: "Uh, sorry, I don't know ... Today's my first day ... I guess I could check with those guys in the kitchen."

Turnover, you see, makes your restaurant a far less inviting place to be. And your customers will show you how they feel about it simply by not returning. So how do you break the cycle?

1. Become a better recruiter so you'll attract more suitable applicants.

2. Become a better interviewer so you can select only the best candidates.

3. Become a better leader so those employees will want to stay.

Unfortunately, it's not quite as simple as 1-2-3. But these three principles did get us thinking of a few *more* ideas that will help solve your turnover problem. On the pages that follow, you'll find 52 great ideas that will help you find, hire and keep the best — and turn the tables on turnover.

HOW TO USE THIS BOOK

We've broken the book down into three chapters:

- Finding the Best
- Hiring the Best
- Keeping the Best

Each of the 52 ideas is presented alongside a variety of related tips, techniques, samples, lists, philosophies, inspirational quotes and incentive ideas. We've designed it this way so it's easier to read and absorb one idea at a time — one a week for a year, if you prefer, or a few ideas each day.

The wealth of great ideas in this book can apply to all segments of the foodservice industry: Full service, family dining, even quick service. Granted, not all restaurant operations are alike. What works for your operation may not work for the one down the street. So think of this as cafeteria-style learning: Take the ideas you like, and leave those not to your taste here in the book.

Once you have finished reading the book, you can put these ideas to work for you by turning to the Action Plan in the back (page 115) and the subsequent "Recruiting," "Interviewing and Hiring" and "Managing for Retention" Strategies (pages 115-117).

"Forget the warm-body syndrome. It takes organized, pleasant and trained individuals to deliver proper and efficient service. It all starts with the hiring process."
—*The American Waiters' Association*

CHAPTER ONE:
Finding the Best

Introduction

Everyone in the restaurant industry agrees that it takes a special kind of person to excel in this business. But it seems that lately these individuals have become rare. It's getting harder to find the warm bodies that you need to get through a shift — let alone good quality employees who care about the success of your business. So you end up hiring whoever — or in some cases, whatever — walks through your door.

Well, contrary to popular belief, there *are* still people out there who will serve you and your guests well, both in the kitchen and in the front of the house. You just need to know where to look for them. Good recruiting is the key to good hiring. Because, if you can't attract a good *quantity* of applicants for your open positions, hiring good *quality* employees becomes impossible.

On the following pages are 18 great ideas for *finding* the best people to meet your operation's needs. You'll learn that the best way to begin any good search for employees is first to decide *who* it is you're looking for. Identifying who the winners are makes it easier to figure out where they hang out. And you'll discover the importance of using a variety of different recruiting methods for all of your different positions. That way you can go to them — wherever they're hiding — instead of waiting for them to come to you.

You're Never Fully Staffed

Recruiting is a philosophy, not a department

If your operation has chronic staffing problems, you know what it means to say, "You're *never* fully staffed!" Every time an employee leaves, it screws up all of your systems, lowers staff morale, drives up costs — and it has a profoundly negative effect on the service you provide your guests.

Some turnover is inevitable in the restaurant business. But if your turnover rate is exceeding the 100 percent mark — turning over every position once in a 365-day period — you'll need to start making some drastic changes. The best way to decrease your high turnover percentage is to learn how to effectively hire the best people and retain them by creating a more positive, fun working environment. All of this, however, takes time.

Meanwhile, you can begin to get the situation under control by treating recruiting as a philosophy, not a department. Commit to *constant* recruiting, because you'll never be able to hire the best possible staff if you can't attract the best possible people to apply at your restaurant. Recruiting is an ongoing process — a year-round job. By limiting your recruiting, you limit the number of qualified candidates to choose from. You may inadvertently eliminate a great hire from consideration — and instead feel forced into hiring a less-than-suitable candidate simply because of a lack of applicants.

That's not to say you should spend thousands of dollars on an endless stream of classified advertising. But you should always be on the lookout for bright, energetic, service-oriented people, whether they come walking through your door or you run into them as you visit other businesses. Once you adopt this mind-set, you'll begin to recognize them everywhere. Seek out new recruiting ideas. Try *everything*. You never know what form of recruiting will gain the most attention from the people you want to attract.

When applicants come to you, don't turn them away because you have no current openings. Who knows what staff changes tomorrow will bring? Every person who requests an application should be given one. If it's in the middle of the dinner rush and a young guest with a bright smile and charming demeanor expresses an interest in a server position, why not spare a few minutes to get to know him or her? You should never be too busy to talk to people who want to work for you. It doesn't have to be a formal interview at this point, just show the person that you're interested. Later when a position opens up, you'll have the application on file.

Time On Your Side

Vary your application times. Your best future employees may be working somewhere else when you want them to apply. So offer more than one time each day to accept applications and conduct interviews. For instance, you may access a larger slice of the labor pool by holding interviews from 5 p.m. to 7 p.m. on Mondays and Tuesdays and 10 a.m. to noon on Saturdays.

2 Personality Counts

Identify your ideal candidate

Develop a written "personality profile" of your ideal candidate, detailing the character traits that would best match the personality of your restaurant. You may have already written something similar that outlines your operation's requirements for work experience and skills — in effect, a job description. A personality profile is something different. It doesn't have to be pages long — in fact, it could be a paragraph included on the job description itself. It should outline *soft* skills, like "detail-oriented," "outgoing," or "adventurous," rather than hard skills like "the ability to perform addition and subtraction."

Creating a personality profile may sound like a simple step — one not worthy of a busy manager's time. But you'd be surprised how many managers make the mistake of hiring the same people — the wrong people — over and over again because they weren't sure what type of personality would provide the best fit for their operation. Candidates can have all the skills and experience you're looking for, but if they don't fit in with your vision of your restaurant, they won't last.

You'll want to create a separate profile for every position in your restaurant — they'll all be slightly different. A dishwasher obviously requires a different personality than a server. The *person* has the personality, not the position. For each position, ask yourself what's really important in a candidate and what basic skills the job requires. Then, decide what type of personality would most likely possess

> "We're looking for personality. We can train for skills. We want people who are enthusiastic, who have pride in their work, who can take charge of a situation without supervision."
>
> —*Duncan Dickson, Director of "Casting," Walt Disney World*

> "It doesn't matter what your résumé says. The main prerequisite is that you're nice."
>
> —*Hal Rosenbluth, author*

those skills. If you have a tough time isolating the ideal personality traits, take a closer look at your successful employees. How are they different from the ones who don't work out?

Once you've completed the personality profile, you're ready to begin looking for candidates that meet those specs. Your first clue's right there on your desk: Read the personality profile again, this time with a different view. Think of *where* you'd find such a candidate. This second reading is often surprisingly helpful. Keep the profile on file so the next time that position opens up, you and others who make hiring decisions will be 100 percent clear about who you're really looking for.

Sample Personality Profile — Server

The ideal server is outgoing and personable. Candidates for this position should have a real "showbiz" personality, undaunted by the feeling of being "on-stage." They should also show a willingness to go the extra mile to provide a great dining experience for every customer and be able to communicate in a positive manner with managers, co-workers and guests. Servers should recognize the job as a sales position and understand that suggestive selling means better customer service.

3 Ad It Up

Tips on effective advertising

> "The will to win is not as important as the will to prepare to win."
>
> —*Bobby Knight, college basketball coach*

Be selective in your advertising. We're in the age of job networking — even in the restaurant industry. These days, fewer and fewer jobs are actually filled through classified advertisements because hirers complain that, even though they get a large number of responses, too few of the applicants are right for the available position. They waste a great deal of time and energy weeding through applications and conducting dead-end interviews to find only a few suitable candidates.

But that's not to say you should give up on classified ads completely. Done well, they could entice a good *quality* of applicants rather than a good quantity of applicants. Just try to choose those outlets that will produce the best candidates at the lowest cost. Place your ad where your best prospective employees are sure to read it. Your advertising dollars may be better spent in community newspapers (such as church flyers, college newspapers, weekly entertainment periodicals or suburban shopping center newspapers) or other specialized periodicals rather than the biggest paper in town.

In your ads, be sure to describe the job in detail and use the right words to express the candidate you're looking for. Look back to the personality profile you created and stress those character traits in your ad. The first questions prospective employees ask are, "Can I do this job?" and "Will I enjoy doing it?" Give prospective employees as much information as possible as early as you can.

Avoid using blind employment ads — those lacking your restaurant's name. They won't generate a good response from the kind of applicants you're trying to attract. And, there may be job seekers who've dined at your restaurant thinking, "Bet it's fun to work here!" but didn't follow through. Once they see the ad, they'll remember.

To boost response to a help-wanted ad, place a "teaser" ad in another section. For example, if you want sales-oriented servers, place your ad under the restaurant category and place a teaser ad under "sales" to attract those sales personalities.

TIP

Sample "teaser" ad:

Wanted: Sales Professionals.

Tired of telemarketing? Dread door-to-door? Want to make more money? We're looking for a few good customer-oriented salespeople to join our team. Our customers come in to buy, not browse, and our salespeople make a 10- to 20- percent commission on everything they sell. If you're friendly, outgoing and personable, apply at Joe's Diner for the best sales job you'll ever have. Please see our ad under "restaurants" for more information.

4 Higher Education

Recruit at colleges

> "Surround yourself with the highest caliber people. Remember that first-rate people hire first-rate people — while second-rate people hire third-rate people."
>
> —Richard M. White, Jr., author

Recruiting at colleges can turn up a lot of desirable candidates. Call a local college's Career Services department — they'll always have a referral or two. Some colleges also have regular job service lines to help their students find summer jobs. Or, contact the college's student newspaper to place a classified ad for your open position. You may get a better response than in the big daily paper.

Or go to the source. If you're looking for a server with strong sales abilities, contact the college's Marketing department. If you're looking for someone who'll feel at ease speaking to your customers, contact the Speech department. If you're looking for outgoing personalities unafraid of the restaurant "showbiz," contact the Drama department. Or seek out a college with a Hospitality curriculum. Lots of people say they enjoy customer service. Hospitality majors have already committed to a career in the industry.

One of the best places to find a good kitchen crew is at a culinary school. These chefs-in-training will appreciate the chance to use what they're learning in school — and they'll add new life to your menu. Many are required to intern a certain number of hours before graduation. You may be able to put them to work part-time before they graduate and keep them full-time afterward. Guarantee them the opportunity to be creative and show their strengths, and you may just keep them for their career.

Once you have college students moonlighting at your restaurant, you're sure to keep them if you're willing to work around their schedules. When you recruit college students, let them know during the interview that you support their efforts toward a higher education. Guarantee time off for preparing for midterms and finals, and allow flexible scheduling throughout the school year, giving students the option to switch shifts or leave early on evenings before big exams.

Fortunately for you, college students' free time runs parallel to most restaurants' busiest times. Keep in touch with your best seasonal employees, and welcome them back for their next break. Before they head back to school in September, let them know that you'd be happy to put them to work during the holiday rush. To keep track, have them each fill out a postcard with their name and school address, then send that postcard to the student as a reminder just before winter, spring and summer breaks.

Stock Up for Summer

Try offering a cash reward, say $100, to those college students you'd like to have back the following season. One way to set up the incentive is to reward those workers who refer at least one other person who will work through the next summer season. Or, you can base the reward on the student's academic achievement. Award bonuses only to workers who maintain a specified grade point average during the school year. Award the bounty after they finish the season, not on the first day they clock in. This is especially effective with students working their way through school. Consider making the check payable directly to their school or college fund.

5 Here's My Card

Use your business cards to recruit

> **"The best people are always working for someone else."**
>
> *—Brett Shone, Senior Management Training Coordinator, Apple South, Inc.*

> **"You were not hired, you were selected."**
>
> *—Jim Veil, General Manager, Ritz-Carlton, to new employees*

You see the signs everywhere: "Now hiring," "Help wanted, inquire within." The turnover crisis in this industry has caused many restaurant operations to go into a perpetual state of advertising — waiting for the perfect employee to waltz through the front door. But the best employees may not always come to you. Sometimes you have to go looking for them.

If you're seeking someone who'll provide consistently good customer service for your guests, don't limit your hiring practices to the usual ads and window banners. Your best prospects may have never considered a career in the restaurant industry. They might be working somewhere else, in another service-related job.

Have you ever come across a smiling, industrious employee at a car wash? How about a friendly representative at a car rental counter? Did your salesperson at that clothing store really "wow" you with exceptional service? These are the kind of people you want working for you, whether they have restaurant experience or not. As is often said: "Hire the smile."

When you find that person, discreetly give him or her your business card and say, "I appreciate your smile and excellent service. If you're ever looking for work, please give me a call." Who knows? Maybe that person has been on the lookout for a part-time income or a whole new line of work. If not, you've at least made his or her day by complimenting the service, and you've also planted a valuable seed. That person may know someone who's looking for work, someone with equal customer service skills, someone who turns out to be the best hiring decision you've ever made. All for the price of a single business card.

Encourage all the managers and assistant managers in your restaurant to keep their eyes peeled for people in the business of providing quality customer service. While you're at it, get the whole staff involved. Consider offering cash bounties to anyone who brings aboard an employee as a result of handing out a business card. One good idea is to split that bounty — say, $50 — between the new employee and the person who made the discovery, provided that the new employee sticks around for at least 60-90 days. You may be surprised by the results!

Top 10 Places To Find Potential Employees

1. Hotel/motel front desks
2. Supermarkets
3. Toy/children's stores
4. Retail clothing stores
5. Convenience stores/gas stations

6. Car washes
7. Video rental stores
8. Car rental counters
9. Copy centers/printing shops
10. Customer service counters at department stores

6 Be Flexible

Don't discourage part-timers

Too many managers confuse "part-time employee" with "part-time commitment." Part-timers are often the best workers, especially homemakers who choose to wait tables two or three nights a week. They come to work smiling and leave happy. Why? Because they actually get tipped to do at your restaurant (serve food and drinks) what they may get indifference for at home.

But they aren't the only ones. College students often have erratic scheduling needs — especially around midterms and finals when they need extra study time. And employees who work at your restaurant for a second income on top of a "real" job may only want to work a few hours a week. By turning away people with non-traditional scheduling needs, you eliminate a large part of the work force. So consider going to a flex-time or job-sharing type of scheduling system.

The key to flex-time scheduling is to look at positions as hours, not shifts. Where there's usually one person covering a particular shift for 40 hours a week, you may have two, three or even four people covering that shift at only a few hours apiece.

Sure, scheduling can become much more of a headache with a job-sharing or flex-time system. The solution? Let those part-timers do their own scheduling. Set up a form of "buddy system" in which three or four employees are responsible for covering a particular shift every week. Let the team work together to set their own schedules and submit it to you each week. Encourage them to come to you only if they have major conflicts. Take it a step further by having the group exchange phone numbers. If one member of that team has a last-minute conflict and can't cover a shift, he or she can network with co-workers to find a replacement.

You'll be out of the loop, which saves you time to focus on other management functions. And you'll decrease the number of no-shows and people quitting because they couldn't get the time off they needed. With part-timers, job-sharing and flex-scheduling, everyone gets just what they want. It translates into more motivated and committed workers who'll stick around.

Power to the Part-Timer

Most waitstaff incentives target sales per month, leaving the part-time employee out of the picture. Try this incentive, based on sales per hour, to get everyone involved. Start by determining each server's sales average per hour for each shift you're open for business, based on figures for the past three months (or an average of four or five random shifts). Divide gross sales by hours worked. Post these base figures so everyone knows where they stand. At the end of each shift, tally everyone's sales per hour. Then, at the end of each week of the contest, post the sales-per-hour averages on a bulletin board. Compare figures to the original ones, noting any improvement or decline. Review performances on an individual basis or at daily pre-shift meetings. At the end of the month, the server whose averages have improved the most on a percentage basis wins.

7 Look Around You

Hiring from within

Before you go to all the trouble and expense of recruiting outside your restaurant, make sure the right candidate for the job isn't already right under your nose — working within your restaurant in another position. The people already working for you who have proven themselves reliable, hardworking and honest may end up being your best choices for your open positions.

Whenever possible, promote and train your best buspeople into server positions. They already know the routine — they see it every shift. Promote food expediters to prep cooks, dishwashers to line cooks and servers to assistant managers. Your employees are already familiar with the tasks involved in other positions within your restaurant — and with the overall environment. Training and orientation will be cut down significantly so there will be a shortened adjustment period from one position to the next.

A "promote-from-within" philosophy not only saves you recruiting time and money, it also breeds loyalty because it provides an incentive for those entry-level workers to perform at the top of their abilities. It shows that you care about the advancement of the people working for you and don't just see them as a number or a position. It's also a good selling point when you have to go outside to hire for positions. People will feel better about accepting an entry-level position if they know there's a chance to move up. This furthers the perception of the restaurant industry as a career — not just a rest stop on

"Our philosophy is to share success with the people who make it happen. It makes everybody think like an owner, which helps them build long-term relationships with customers and influences them to do things in an efficient way."

—Emily Ericsen, Vice President of Human Resources, Starbucks Coffee Company

the way to bigger and better things. Your staff's productivity will increase and so will the overall morale.

Conversely, think of the morale problems caused by recruiting someone from the outside to fill a job that could be filled by someone already working for the restaurant. It will undoubtedly cause friction, and can often make it difficult for the new person to perform successfully. Even worse, by hiring someone from the outside, you risk losing a qualified employee who was passed over.

Keep It Fair

Once you decide to adopt a promote-from-within philosophy, set up policies to keep it fair. Here are some tips for setting up a level playing field:

- **Begin the process during orientation.** Tell every new hire: "If you're ever interested in another position, let a manager know. We'll do everything we can to prepare you."

- **Post job openings on an employee bulletin board.** Set policies for submitting applications. Carefully consider every application. The employee may not be ready for the job now, but you can help them better prepare for it.

- **Review each employee's advancement goals at evaluations.** Help them to prepare goal statements outlining the steps they'll take to get prepared.

- **Cross-train employees in the new positions** — before there's an opening. That way, they'll be trained and ready to go when a position opens.

⑧ Birds of a Feather...

Have your staff help you recruit

Once you've hired four or five good people, hire their friends and contacts. Forget the outdated advice "never consider friends or family for hiring." This makes no more sense than hiring people based only on age, gender, ethnicity or schooling. Good people are good people. Start with a solid foundation, then build from it.

When you hire a group of people who know each other, much of the team-building is already done for you. In a friendlier environment, staff members will help one another to get the job done — and not because they have to. You'll decrease the chances of staff members not getting along.

And you'll end up with a solid team made up of similar personalities, which, in turn, will help your restaurant develop its own distinct personality. It will create an atmosphere that will attract more guests — a fun and friendly environment where people want to hang out.

To help create this environment, post job openings internally and get your staff to help you recruit by offering a bounty for referring their friends. For instance, if a server recommends someone for an open position, and that new hire stays at least 60-90 days and excels in his or her service and sales, give that server a reward for the referral. Rewards can include cash, gift certificates for dinners at other restaurants or merchandise.

"You don't try to build character in a team, you eliminate people who don't have character."

—Paul Brown, Cleveland Browns founder

Your employees have a lot to gain from recommending people they know will do a great job since they will have to work with them. And they have just as much to lose by recommending marginal people.

TIP Family Ties

Mom-and-Pop operations may have always had it right — if you want to hire good people, keep it in the family. In many cases, excellent servers are the products of a happy, hospitable home environment. So the question arises, "Are there any more at home like you?" If there are, shouldn't their brothers, sisters, cousins, nieces and nephews be working at your place, too?

9 Strength in Numbers

Open house/group interviews

> "To get to the top of the heap, first you must have a heap."
> —Gene Perret

Hold an open house or group interview. It's a recruiting method that's especially effective for grand openings or if you need to fill several positions at once. Open houses take a little extra work in the planning stages than your typical interview, but you may find the work worthwhile since the relaxed, informal atmosphere lets you get to know many applicants at once and won't make unsuitable applicants feel rejected if they're not invited to an interview.

Schedule open houses to accommodate as many applicants as possible. Use regular recruiting methods to reach potential applicants: ads, flyers, etc. Review applications in your file and invite walk-ins, as well. Refer to the session as an "open house," not an "interview" or a "screening."

To prepare, create interview invitations to give to applicants who make round two. Set aside blocks of time (at different times of day) in your schedule for interviews. Create a list of 50 open-ended interview questions — some easier, some tougher behavior-based questions. Schedule one manager for every seven or eight applicants attending.

To conduct an open house, first welcome everyone, introduce yourself and explain the purpose of inviting them: *"It's a great way for us to get to know you and for you to get to know us in a casual, no-pressure atmosphere."* Ask how many have eaten at your restaurant. Describe your restaurant's menu, style of service and atmosphere. Pass out applications and copies of job descriptions. Review the job descriptions out loud and have everyone sign a form that states they are aware of the essential functions of the job.

Then, ask applicants, *"What would you like to discover about us?"* Write their questions on a flip chart. Topics may include wages, benefits, scheduling, management philosophies and opportunities for advancement. You may want to prepare and memorize a brief explanation for each topic ahead of time. If the group doesn't bring up a topic, bring it up yourself.

Then break everyone into groups and pass out copies of the questions. Go around the circle having applicants take turns answering questions. Keep it fun, conversational and upbeat so it won't be intimidating. Continue through all of the questions until everyone's had a turn. Finally, thank everyone for coming and tell them: "I will walk each of you out." As you walk each participant to the door, say: "If you haven't heard from us in 24 hours, we've selected another applicant" or invite the applicant to return for a one-on-one interview.

Open-Door Policy

If you're going to hold an open house or group interview, be sure you understand the legal implications that come with it. Some applicants may mistakenly view open houses as your attempt to find just those "looks" that suit your operation. By inviting a large group of applicants to participate, you're giving the impression that everyone has the same shot at available positions. So be prepared to give serious consideration to *every* applicant who walks through the door, regardless of race, color, creed, sex, national origin, age, disability or other protected status. Be sure you understand and adhere to the current guidelines of the Americans with Disabilities Act. And be especially careful not to single out or exclude anyone during the group interview.

10 They're Worth It

Offer wage guarantees

Operators nationwide report that their kitchen-crew positions turn over more than any other position in the restaurant. It's a dangerous phenomenon for the industry when you consider that these hardworking folk are the heart of any good restaurant operation. You can't really continue to exist without them. Yet, too often they are the most under-appreciated members of the staff.

And since they aren't tipped employees, there isn't much incentive to keep them from jumping to the competition. Indeed, experienced kitchen staffers say their usual criteria for taking a job is a fun working environment where they feel appreciated and are rewarded for their hard work.

So it stands to reason that the best way to *attract* the very best kitchen staffers and get them to apply at your restaurant is to promise them a better work atmosphere, more recognition and, most important, a more competitive wage. This added bonus may be all that it takes to convince them to come to work for you. When you run classified ads for kitchen positions, promise that their starting wage will "meet or beat" whatever wage they're currently receiving. Good news travels fast in this business!

Many operators, though, let their penny-pinching instincts take over and just hope their kitchen crew will stick around at the industry's standard wage rate. It's understandable, what with the high costs of running a restaurant these days. But consider how much *more* you're spending to

> "Pay peanuts and you get monkeys."
> —*Anonymous*

> "When an employee tells you it's the principle of the thing and not the money, it's the money."
> —*Jean Goetz*

recruit and train new employees every time a kitchen staffer decides to leave. You'll find that this small investment pays off big in the long run with happier kitchen employees who'll want to stay.

Avoid a Wage Rage

If you're going to offer new hires a little something extra in pay, you'd better be sure that you won't alienate those faithful employees already working for you. Always assume that the salary of a new employee will become public knowledge. People talk. So if you've agreed to pay that new employee more than what other kitchen-crew members in comparable positions are making, think again. You may be risking the loss of a faithful employee by showing more appreciation to a new hire. Before you set a higher wage for the new employee, consider a raise for those already there. Expensive? Maybe, but think of what you stand to lose.

Recruiting on the Road

> "Go as far as you can see, and when you get there you will see farther."
>
> —*Early American Proverb*

Recruit at off-site special events

If you're running out of ideas for getting applicants through your restaurant's doors, recruit at off-site special events. Not only are these events great marketing vehicles for attaining new customers, they're also great recruiting methods for reaching potential applicants who may live in other parts of your city or region. This method is especially effective for "destination" operations located in out-of-the-way areas where there are few passers-by to take notice of "Help Wanted" signs in the windows.

Whenever you take your restaurant show on the road for food festivals, trade shows or other special events, be sure to bring along a stack of applications and business cards. Put together a collage of snapshots of your employees — serving, smiling and having a great time at work. Put a teaser headline on the poster, like "Look like fun? Ask us about how *you* can be part of the team."

Let all your booth staffers know about available positions and your restaurant's requirements for work experience. Encourage those staffers to talk to visitors not only about visiting the restaurant as diners, but also visiting the restaurant as applicants.

Music festivals and sporting events are great sites for finding server personalities. Culinary trade shows are often great sources for recruiting kitchen staffers. And industry seminars could provide some potential manager trainees.

You may also consider renting booth space at career fairs. It's one of the few venues where almost every participant is a potential applicant. Everyone there is looking for a new career opportunity!

Be sure to bring along plenty of written materials about your restaurant: brochures for special events, menus, maybe even a brochure that highlights the people working for you. Consider providing free food samples to attract more potential applicants to your booth. Once you have their attention, you can speak more intimately about the industry and the career potential that comes with it.

Special Events

Any time your operation participates in such off-site special events as those listed below, bring along a stack of applications.

Restaurant association trade shows	State/county fairs	Parades
Nonprofit fund-raisers	Food festivals	Political rallies
Beer festivals and tastings	Outdoor concerts	Grand openings
Chili cook-offs	Sporting events	Culinary festivals
Art shows	Career fairs	Wine-tasting events
Rodeos/stock shows	Industry seminars	Civic celebrations

12 No Cloning Around

Don't look for a clone of yourself

Few managers will admit to the fact that what they really want in an employee is someone who thinks and feels exactly the way they do. It's human nature to want to surround yourself with similar personalities — people whose philosophies, work ethics and backgrounds are the same as your own. But be careful. By eliminating people who are different from yourself, you're eliminating the chance for creative solutions to your biggest problems and new ideas for the future. No business can function if everyone thinks exactly alike. Creative solutions require thinking "outside the box."

It's a pattern you'll especially want to avoid when you're hiring for manager and management trainee positions. These are the people who lead the rest of your staff. And you'll never be able to maintain an entire staff of identical personalities in the restaurant business. Every employee within your operation will require a different management style. By diversifying your management force, you'll provide stronger leadership for the overall team.

And, think of it this way: If you're hiring only those candidates with strengths identical to your own, you may also be hiring people with identical weaknesses. Seek out people who can do what you can't. This balance of personalities will fill in the gaps and strengthen the overall operation.

When you're recruiting, think about how you were hired — the skills and experience that got you there. Then look elsewhere to find employees. If you came up through the ranks of a large corporate operation with hundreds of units, look for management trainees who came up through one-unit independents. Advertise in different regions than your own — maybe even in different states. You may find someone far away with a different management style who's looking for a change of scenery.

You may even consider looking for candidates with different backgrounds altogether. So what if a candidate has never managed a restaurant before? Maybe they've managed a clothing store. Different set of problems. Different set of solutions — maybe some that will work for you.

Opposites Attract

If you want to build a balanced management team, look for personalities that complement each other. It requires looking closely at your own personality, admitting to your own weaknesses and choosing people who are different from yourself.

If your management style is:	Look for someone whose style is more:
Logical, precise and meticulous	Creative, theoretical and impulsive
Strict, critical and demanding	Tolerant, motivational and understanding
Careful, practical and down to earth	Inventive, conceptual and easygoing

B Be Creative

Recruiting where the competition isn't

If you're constantly understaffed and operate in an area with a shrinking labor pool, you'll need an arsenal of different recruiting weapons to keep up with your needs. The only way to ward off the turnover blues? Try *anything* and *everything* to get the message out there that you need good people. Here are a few creative ideas that'll help:

Advertise in movie theaters. You'll be able to deliver your job-opening message to a captive audience of your best potential applicants — right before the movie previews at the local cineplex. This can be a costly method, but you'll find that it produces a significant number of applicants.

Contact a theater group or comedy club. Aspiring actors and entertainers are often looking for a second income. They may require some alternative scheduling needs — evenings off for their other job — but given the right accommodations, they may just stick with you until they're "discovered."

Hold a weekend mini job fair at the local mall. You can rent tables or empty storefronts in malls any weekend. Why not take advantage of all that traffic to distribute applications or promote job openings? Be where the people are.

Consider PTA periodicals for placing classified ads. You'll reach PTA moms and dads who can pass the message on to their older children, or maybe a homemaker or two looking for a second income. Don't forget church bulletins and church youth groups as a source. And you may even try

> "The significant problems we face cannot be solved at the same level of thinking you were at when you created them."
>
> —*Albert Einstein*

advertising in senior citizen newsletters — seniors may have children or grandchildren who are looking for work. Or hire the seniors themselves if you want friendly, hard workers that will appreciate the chance to be active in a youth-oriented atmosphere. Mixing up generations allows both ends of the age spectrum to learn from each other.

TIP

Post colorful, creative flyers at:

Youth group halls	**College student union bulletin boards**
Youth sports organizations	**Grocery stores**
Arcades	**Gyms/Health clubs**
Fraternity/sorority houses	**College bars**
Military bulletin boards	**Apartment complexes**
Laundromats	**Video stores**
Senior centers	**Community recreation centers**

14 Go High Tech!

Recruiting on the Internet

If you're looking to expand your recruiting power beyond the usual classified ads, the Internet is the newest and fastest-growing medium for career networking. It's not just for computer-related jobs anymore. Many businesses have already embarked on the information superhighway to find good employees, and the restaurant industry can't be far behind. Since users can now order pizzas on-line, couldn't they also hear about your job openings?

Once you've braved the leap onto the Net, you'll see that the advertising advantages are clear. For the cost of a week's advertising in your local newspaper, you can post your message around the world, 24 hours a day, to an ever-increasing audience. Commercial services such as America Online, CompuServe, Prodigy and Genie include classified and help-wanted databases.

The Internet contains discussion groups (known as newsgroups, forums, clubs, bulletin boards, roundtables or special-interest groups) that appeal to specific interests — including job-hunting. In the various "jobs-offered" databases, employment notices are listed by country, state and city first, then by job description (such as "restaurant management"). For your upper-management positions, you'll be able to review résumés from applicants across the country who may already be planning a move to your area.

Of course, people seeking server positions are less likely to relocate for a job. For this, there are also discussion groups dedicated to particular cities and local areas, and these often include help-wanted sections. Consider posting your notice for servers here, especially if you're located near a university. Many colleges offer students free Internet access.

One of the most rapidly growing on-line services is the World Wide Web. Here, any business or individual can set up a Web page — a fact sheet that can include everything from promotional information to the fanciest graphics and even photos of your restaurant, available to anyone at the touch of a button. Not only can you reach prospective employees this way, but potential customers as well!

TIP

Net Etiquette

A few words of caution before you go head-hunting on-line: Prior to advertising on any discussion group, take the time to read the messages that are already there to make sure you're in the right place. Posting a message in an inappropriate area (for instance, a commercial advertisement in a newsgroup dedicated to casual conversation) may result in your getting "flamed" — harassed and insulted by other users. And you could even wind up losing your Net account if enough people complain to the system administrator. Also, remember that initial responses to your on-line ad will most likely be via E-mail, which is usually less formal than a letter or even a phone call.

15 The Power of Perks

Be the preferred employer by offering creative perks

A drive down any street in America is proof of just how competitive the restaurant industry is these days. But not only are you competing for customers, you're competing for good employees. As the labor force continues to shrink, operators in competitive areas see an increasing need to offer something different. Become the preferred employer by offering special perks that your competition doesn't. Be sure to emphasize these perks in every classified ad.

Warning: Some of the following perk ideas will cost you a few extra bucks in the short run. But they pay off big in the long run with happy employees who want to stick around. By attracting the best employees and providing them with incentives to stay, you cut down on all the extra costs of constant recruiting, hiring and training new employees.

One reason restaurant positions aren't viewed as "real jobs" is that few operations offer the type of perks that corporate America offers. Consider offering long-term employees (say after six months to a year on the job) educational reimbursements, profit sharing, a company-matched 401(k) plan or a promote-from-within philosophy. Another criterion people cite for avoiding careers in the restaurant industry is its aversion to covering health insurance. It's an expensive gesture, but one that will draw a steady stream of applicants. If you simply can't afford full coverage, consider offering partial coverage. It's still more than most of your competitors offer.

> "In addition to treating people fairly and with respect, I'm a firm believer in offering a great new hire a unique benefit that my competitors can't offer them."
>
> —*Dennis J. Porter, Manager, Embers Restaurant*

Most restaurant jobs are perfect for young, unattached people who don't want long-term commitments and don't have families to support. But you can attract more mature employees by helping them maintain their growing families. Providing day-care assistance is one way to help. And offering two weeks paid maternity leave or flex-time/job-sharing options will allow mothers to spend more time at home.

Today's fitness-conscious work force would jump at the offer of a free health club membership. But set up the incentive with a catch: Only pay for it if it's used. Here's how: Approach a local health club with dinner gift certificates to your restaurant in trade for keeping track of your employees' workouts. Provide them with a chart of participant names. Have the employee pay the initial six-month membership fee. After six months, tally up weekly averages. If the employee works out three times per week, you reimburse half. Four times per week pays three-quarters. And five times per week earns full reimbursement, which participants can put toward their next six-month membership fee.

Perks for Pennies

So maybe you can't afford a comprehensive benefits package and expensive perks. Every little bit helps! Try advertising some of these unusual — and inexpensive — perks to attract more applicants:

Free coffee for life	**A one-month all-you-can-ride bus pass**
Half-price meals	**A free pair of work shoes/uniform**
Write your own schedule for a month	**Trade out dinner gift certificates with popular clothing stores and give new hires $20 gift certificates to use as they wish after they've finished their first week of training.**

16 The Young and the Restless

Be a volunteer speaker at high schools and colleges

All too often, young people in this country view jobs in the restaurant business as interim positions — a place to pause for a spell while planning *real* careers. By contrast, Europeans view restaurant jobs as lifelong vocations. Indeed, men and women there consider restaurant crafts to be positions of service with fine traditions to uphold and important skills to be learned and honed.

One way to help change the American perception is to spread a positive message about restaurant careers to the country's young people. Volunteer to speak at high school and college classes and career fairs. Teens are on the threshold of planning their careers. If you can get to them early, you may be able to change that negative perception about the industry before it's too late.

Use your classroom time to emphasize the fun nature of this business. Demonstrate your own pride in the industry — describe why you chose your career and how you moved into your current position. Emphasize the many opportunities for career growth — from busperson to server to assistant manager to general manager or food expediter to prep cook to chef to kitchen manager. You may even inspire an audience member to open his or her *own* restaurant someday.

Describe the earning potential in the industry. Sure, the money's not as good as, say, a career as an engineer or a doctor. But for those young people who can't afford a college education — or are in the process of getting one — the money's better than they'd earn in a lot of other fields. More important, in an age of corporate downsizing and rising unemployment, you can assure your young audience that there will *always* be jobs available in the restaurant industry.

Bring along a folder of applications to pass out and describe the entry-level positions now open in your restaurant. Encourage members of the audience to give it a shot, at least while they're still in school. A restaurant is, after all, one of the only types of businesses that can give inexperienced 16-year-olds the opportunity to earn spending money while teaching them skills that can support them for a lifetime.

TIP

Investing in the Future

Consider offering $500 to $1,000 in college tuition scholarships for employees who demonstrate a desire for a career in hospitality or restaurant management. Set it up so only employees who've been with your restaurant for at least six continuous months and have demonstrated above-average performance on the job are eligible. As their education continues, become a mentor by taking the time to explain your management functions. Challenge those students by letting them take on a few of your management tasks. It will free up your time and provide a valuable on-the-job education for the management future of the industry.

17 Call in the Feds

Look to government agencies as recruiting sources

Government agencies are an often-overlooked recruiting source. It's too bad, since they can provide some highly capable workers who are anxious to prove their self-worth on the job. Don't overlook these agencies — especially for your hard-to-fill positions! The staffs at these agencies work diligently, often for free, to place people in jobs. You'll appreciate all the extra help that allows you to focus on other management functions. And, these agencies often provide people who'll work harder for you than the average high school or college student because they appreciate the opportunity more.

By making an effort to give under-employed sectors of society a shot, you will not only receive the extra help you need, but also further emphasize your operation's positive presence in the community. This good deed can provide some great revenue-generating public relations — maybe even a spot on the evening news.

More important, though, by providing these displaced workers with the right opportunities, training and structured support, they may just become your restaurant's most loyal and motivated employees — a step in the right direction for solving your turnover problem. And these workers will serve as an inspiration to everyone on your staff, which can make everyone work harder. So maybe they aren't all young college students in perfect physical condition. If they can perform the essential functions of the job, they may just outwork your adolescent scholars.

"Progress involves risk. You can't steal second base and keep your foot on first."

—Rick Van Warner, Editor, Nation's Restaurant News

Start with the local job service agency and the unemployment office. Don't buy into the mind-set that the unemployed don't *want* to work. With all the downsizing in recent years, many of the unemployed are simply looking for a second chance in life. On that note, if you hear on the news that a large corporation has been forced into major layoffs, call their personnel office. They'll probably be acting as an out-placement office and be happy to send you a few referrals.

Regularly inform local civic, youth and senior citizen groups and professional, nonprofit organizations of your job opportunities. You can register at a lot of different agencies — free of charge.

TIP

Do a Good Deed

Look to these often overlooked sources for your hard-to-fill positions:

- **Social Services**
- **State and local unemployment offices**
- **Vocational rehabilitation centers**
- **Division of Family Services**
- **Department of Veterans' Affairs**

18 The Gang's All Here

Good customers make great employees

The turnover crisis in this industry has worked many restaurant operators into a recruiting frenzy, causing them to spend a great deal of money and time looking all over creation for the right people. Sometimes, though, the right people may be walking through your front door. Good customers often make great employees. They know your business, they know your menu — and they've shown you, through their patronage, that they like the overall personality of your restaurant. Perhaps they'd like to come to work for you? Well, you'll never know for sure unless you *ask*!

Don't give up on the tried-and-true "help wanted, apply within" banner on the premises, which so many restaurant operators have come to reject. Being understaffed is nothing to be ashamed of! The people who will see the signs and apply are the people who likely know your restaurant best — the customers. Just give this old method a new twist: Print creative brochures featuring pictures of your fun and happy staff serving and smiling. Or hang a brightly colored banner above the bar that sings the praises of working in your restaurant.

Or, go to your database. Your marketing mailing list is made up of the names and addresses of your best customers. Since you frequently send out information on upcoming promotions, next time include a note addressed to their teenage sons or daughters who may be looking for work. You won't have to spend anything on

"The best parachute folders are the ones who jump themselves."
—*Dwight D. Eisenhower*

extra postage. And you'll get the parents — who're already sold on your restaurant — to help you recruit their kids!

The Lunch Club

Quick-service is the segment of the foodservice industry that experiences the worst of the industry's turnover crisis. It's hard to get good people to stay — especially at minimum wage. So if you run a quick-service operation, you'll need to try just about anything to keep fully staffed. If your operation is situated near a high school, you see hundreds of potential employees *every day*, especially at lunchtime. Make an effort to get to know those regulars who flash a bright smile and a charming demeanor. Those regulars often make the best employees. You already know that they live nearby, that they like your food and, based on your conversations with them, that they'll be personable with your customers. Plus, offer them half-priced meals, and they may just stay with you until graduation.

"At our restaurant,
we have two criteria
for new employees:
They must be alive
and they must be
from this planet."
*—Anonymous Restaurant
Manager*

CHAPTER TWO:
Hiring the Best

Introduction

What's the best way to go about choosing the best applicants for your open positions? You could review a few applications and head to the local fortune teller for a Tarot card reading. It's a risky method, but no more risky than going with your "gut instincts" as many operators do.

You can never be 100-percent sure of hiring the "right" person. A job application can tell you a lot about the past, but it cannot predict the future. You'll have much more hiring success if you can use that application as only a starting point to help you uncover more information about the applicant's skills, capabilities and attitudes.

And there's still no better way to get that information than the traditional job interview. On the following pages we'll let you in on 17 great ways you can improve your interviewing skills, which will improve your odds of finding that perfect match. You'll learn great techniques for getting organized, putting the applicant at ease and asking the right questions to find out the most telling information — as well as how to read between the lines to discern what the applicant *isn't* telling. So forget the fortune teller, ignore your "gut" — welcome to "The Interview."

19 First Impressions

Treat applicants as you would treat guests

When applicants come in to fill out an application, it could be their first visit to your restaurant. First impressions are critical! Not only are you deciding whether to hire them, they're deciding whether they want to work for you.

Applicants are more than potential employees — they're also potential guests. How they're treated could determine whether they patronize your restaurant, even if they don't get the job. Be sure that you and your entire staff treat applicants with the same courtesy and respect you'd show to guests.

The person up front — whether it be a manager, greeter or server — should be taught to give an application form to *anyone* that inquires about employment, regardless of race, color, creed, sex, national origin, age, disability or other protected status. That's the law according to most state, federal and local equal opportunity commissions.

Giving applications to everyone who asks is a good idea anyway, even if you don't have any positions open right now. You're never fully staffed! If your restaurant has a chronic turnover problem, you'll want to maintain a full file of applications to select from should a position open unexpectedly. It's also good PR, sending a positive message to guests and potential employees that you always appreciate opportunities to hear from qualified applicants, whether you're currently hiring or not.

> "Eighty percent of the customers' problems are caused by bad systems, not bad people."
>
> —*John Goodman, President, Tarp Inc.*

Train your greeters or cashiers to review applications and schedule interviews — or extend invitations to open houses. Make certain that greeters or cashiers always have a current schedule of times when managers are available to interview. And be sure that everyone who answers the phone is familiar with the positions currently open in your restaurant should a caller inquire. Every caller should be told that "We're always accepting applications" and given the best time to come in to complete one.

Application forms should always be clean and legible. Imagine the impression a candidate gets when asked to fill out an application form that's been photocopied 600 times and has coffee stains on it. You could turn some good people away by appearing sloppy and disorganized during this critical first impression. Update your application form quarterly with relevant legal revisions or categories.

TIP Essay Tests

Consider adding an essay question to the end of your restaurant's regular employment application, asking applicants about their views on customer service, suggestive selling or teamwork. By design, most job applications tell you little about the applicant's personality, attitudes and motivations. Their answers to your essay questions will set them apart from other applicants, allowing you to see how they formulate thoughts and how well they communicate their feelings. It's a valuable step that can help you decide, when reviewing applications, which applicants to invite in for interviews.

20 Great Expectations

Review job descriptions in detail with applicants

Staple a detailed job description to the application form. That way candidates will know, before an interview even takes place, what will be expected of them should they be selected. If a candidate is already intimidated after reviewing the job description, he or she may choose to bow out of consideration. During the interview, go over the job description and ask candidates if they have any questions or concerns — do they feel they're up to the challenge?

> "As we say in the sewer, if you're not prepared to go all the way, don't put your boots on in the first place."
>
> —*Ed Norton, The Honeymooners*

Of course, none of this is possible if you don't have job descriptions created for every position in your restaurant. The job description's purpose of telling the employee what to expect on the job is actually secondary. The real reason you need job descriptions is so you and other managers are 100 percent clear about who's responsible for what. It will force you to identify all the tasks and responsibilities each individual job involves.

Don't forget that your job descriptions should include not only tasks but expectations, and that they may be looked to as performance standards should you need to discipline or terminate an employee. For instance, you may expect dishwashers to complete the *tasks* of operating the dishwashing machine and unloading bus tubs, but you also *expect* them to work safely, minimize breakage and maintain all of the equipment. Likewise, if you expect servers to "suggestively sell" menu items, your job description should reflect this expectation.

Be careful not to make it so overly detailed and limited in scope that it leaves no room for flexibility in making work assignments. A job description longer than one page is probably too detailed. Be honest. Some employers detail requirements for skills and experience beyond what's really necessary. Others minimize job specs so they can hire at a low salary, then crank up demands later.

All of your job descriptions should comply with the Americans with Disabilities Act of 1990, detailing the essential functions of the job including minimum physical requirements. However, don't put strenuous physical requirements in the job description just because it's possible the employee may have to perform a particular function. Instead, the functions should reflect the actual practices in your restaurant. Run all of the job descriptions through legal counsel and be sure you're aware of what interview questions are acceptable in the eyes of the A.D.A. to avoid a lawsuit.

Sample Job Description: Server

The purpose of this position is to provide timely service that enhances guests' dining experiences. Servers are expected to greet guests; take food/drink orders; garnish and serve food/drinks; carry trays; ensure food/drink items meet guests' satisfaction; remove dishes/glasses, trash; refill beverages; enter orders on a POS register; process payment for guests' checks; load and unload bus tubs; sanitize tables and chairs; reset tables; restock service stations; sweep/mop floor. Servers are expected to complete these tasks in a timely and safe manner. Essential functions require the following abilities: Able to see at a distance and at close range; able to hear in one or both ears; able to read, write and perform addition/subtraction; able to use fingers and hands to carry trays, write, operate equipment; able to bend, lift, reach, climb, walk and stand for up to eight hours.

21 Be Prepared

Improve your interviewing skills

The key to better managing your labor costs is to turn over the applicants, not the employees. How? Become a better interviewer. The most important part of any interview comes in the planning. Being well prepared will send a clear message to applicants that you're serious about finding only the best people to work in your restaurant.

Conducting a good interview is hard work — harder than many hirers realize. Too often they ask a few questions about what they see on the application and then use "gut instincts" to make the final decision on the spot. Sure, intuition plays a role in hiring, but don't use it to draw immediate conclusions about the candidate. Instead, use it to guide your *questioning*. Leave the analysis for later and concentrate on getting to know the applicant.

In planning for the interview, there are three questions you'll need to ask *yourself* before you decide what to ask the *applicant*: 1. "What is the employee going to be asked to do?" 2. "What behaviors, attitudes and aptitudes are required to fit our restaurant's needs?" and 3. "What specific things do I need to find out about each candidate in order to make the right match?"

Use your answers to those questions to develop a list of specific questions for each interview. Write them down in advance. That's not to say you can't ask anything else, but use this list as an outline and ask additional questions if you're curious about something the applicant brings up. As you develop your list, select an equal amount of questions from three

> **"When hiring, do you interview 27 people to find the right person? Or do you interview only once and hire the same person 27 times?"**
>
> *— Len Schlesinger, Harvard Business School professor and author*

categories: Experience/skills, intelligence/aptitude and personality/attitude questions. (You'll find samples of each later in this book.)

Once your list of questions is prepared, you're ready to begin. But just having a list doesn't mean the interview has to be formal. Concentrate on maintaining a *conversation*. Most people hate job interviews because the formality makes the process artificial, awkward and uncomfortable. Once you realize this, though, you'll be able to counteract it. The best way to get candidates to feel comfortable and set aside their interviewing fears is to do the same. Behave naturally. Make small talk first. Don't use trick questions, amateur psychoanalysis or pressure tactics. A candidate who is not playing a role is much more likely to divulge the useful information you'll need to make the right decision. Remember, there are no right or wrong answers. Get acquainted with the *person*.

An Interview Agenda

- Greet the applicant and put him or her at ease with small talk.

- Explain what you hope to accomplish with the interview.

- Tell the applicant that you'll be taking brief notes.

- Ask questions from a prepared question list.

- Follow the 80/20 rule: Let the applicant do 80 percent of the talking — you should only speak 20 percent of the time.

- Review the job description. Answer any questions the applicant may have.

- Finish by explaining your timetable and the next step in the hiring process.

22 Been There, Done That

Questions that reveal experience/skills

> "Like my old shop teacher used to say, 'Find out what you don't do well, and don't do it.'"
>
> —*Bob Snyder*

The obvious place to start your questioning is to determine if the candidate has the basic skills to do the job. Assemble a list of questions designed to shed more light on the candidate's background than what appears on the application. Experience, however, should not be your *only* selection criterion. Use it as a starting point since these questions are easy both to ask and to answer. Talking about the past is usually less threatening for the interviewee than talking about the present, so it helps the applicant relax.

First ask specific background questions — especially things that are unclear on the application. Ask if the position listed under previous experience is the one they were hired for or did they receive a promotion. Then, delve into questions about the applicant's specific skills and knowledge. These will differ from work history questions because you'll want the applicant to elaborate on specific work functions. *"What was a typical day like?" "What tasks took up most of your time?"* Don't assume that because a candidate had a certain title, he or she had full responsibility for the tasks normally associated with that title.

It's also important to ask what tasks the candidate likes or dislikes doing, not only because people are invariably better at performing the tasks they enjoy, but also because people who don't like what they do rarely last long on the job. Better to find out during the interview than after you hire. So ask questions like *"What was the best part of the job? The worst?"* Here are a few more good questions to consider:

"What do you think it takes to be successful in the restaurant business?" This is a less-threatening form of the old *"What are your strengths/weaknesses?"* question. Most people will emphasize their own strengths — anything not mentioned may be a weakness. Follow up that question with *"Would you say you possess those qualities?"* Of course the applicant will say yes, but ask for examples. Then ask, *"What areas do you feel you'd like to get better at?"* The answer to this will indicate the applicant's estimation of his or her own weaknesses. And, should he or she be hired, you'll have a clear direction for the employee's training.

Ask *"What sort of quality standards were you required to follow in your last job?"* to see if the applicant's employers held him or her accountable for mistakes. Follow up with: *"Describe a situation in which you were successful in meeting them."* And *"Describe a situation in which you were unsuccessful."* Also ask performance-based questions like *"Tell me about the busiest shift you've ever worked."*

TIP

Who's the Boss?

"What is your boss's title and what are your boss's functions?" For applications that detail so many tasks and responsibilities that even Superman or Wonder Woman couldn't perform them all on a regular shift, this question will indicate just how much the candidate *really* did and discourage an exaggeration of the importance of those functions. If the applicant tells you the boss did nothing, ask for elaboration. You'll find it's rarely true. It's also important to learn early on if a candidate really doesn't know or care what the boss did. Such apathy indicates a lack of interest in the "big picture."

23 What Do You Know?

Questions that reveal intelligence/aptitude

> "Hire people smarter than you, and get out of their way."
> —*Howard Schultz, Chief Executive, Starbucks Coffee*

You don't need to be a Mensa member to work in a restaurant, but there is a certain degree of basic intelligence required to excel. Server candidates, for example, should be able to think on their feet in difficult situations. Cooks should demonstrate an ability to plan ahead. You'll usually gain a clear view of a candidate's general intelligence and aptitude from the way he or she answers questions, but you should still ask a few questions that reveal how bright and capable the candidate is. You're not necessarily looking for substance in their answers. Look for the ability to formulate thoughts under pressure. Here are a few good questions to ask:

"What do you do when you're having trouble solving a problem?" Is the candidate afraid to ask others for help or advice? Is the candidate more action-oriented or analytical? Also ask: *"How would you go about turning the following negative situation into a positive one?"* Give an example of a situation that could occur on the job. Would they run for a manager or try to solve the problem on their own?

"How do you plan your day?" Does the candidate make lists, get organized and get right at things or does he or she "Just go with the flow..."?

"What should your current (or former) employer do to be more successful?" Does the candidate bad-mouth the employer? Is the candidate able to see his or her own role in the improvement of the restaurant? Also ask: *"What do*

you think are the most serious problems facing the restaurant business today?" The answer will reveal if the candidate is in tune to the big picture. Candidates who can't answer this question at all may be something to be concerned about — especially if they list previous restaurant experience on their application. You'll want the people working for you to understand your operational, marketing and financial challenges.

And, finally, ask: *"What can you do that others who might get this position probably can't do?"* and *"If I were working for you, how would you help me succeed?"* If you have two candidates that seem equally qualified, the answers to these two questions may be the deciding factors.

TIP Go for the Goal

"What are your goals for the next two years?" This may seem like an odd question to ask someone interviewing for a position in the restaurant industry since not everyone plans to make a career out of this business. But ask it anyway. You're not necessarily looking for someone who'll answer: "I plan to be working at this restaurant." You want someone who's able to think things through, who's able to plan ahead and who knows what he or she wants out of life. It's not only a good indication of a candidate's intelligence — it's a sign of self-confidence.

24 Personality Plus

Questions that reveal personality/attitude

Everyone in this industry agrees that it takes a certain type of personality to succeed in the restaurant business. The hours are different. You're working while everyone else is playing. The pay varies. The pace is quicker. Insanity sometimes rules. And when things speed up, emotions can run high. If you're trying to fill a position that requires a certain personality and attitude, you have to give each applicant a chance to reveal his or her personality and attitude by asking them the right questions. Here are a few good ones:

"Why are you interested in working for us?" Is the candidate genuinely interested in your restaurant or merely looking for *any* job? If they know a lot about your restaurant — even know people who already work for you — they will probably fit your personality type.

"Describe your biggest frustrations working in the restaurant business." Answers will reveal how well candidates know themselves, and how comfortable they are revealing weaknesses — areas that may need coaching later if the applicant is hired.

"If you saw someone on the street that you thought you recognized, but weren't quite sure, what would you do?" Extroverted people would walk right up and make the effort. Introverts would "Just keep walking ... wait and see if they recognize me." Which candidate would you want interacting with your guests?

"What are some of the reasons for the successes in your life?" Candidates with strong, gregarious personalities will usually spout off a list of their traits: "My outgoing personality, my optimism, my positive self-image, my desire to succeed." Detail-oriented personalities will usually mention strengths, skills and specific steps toward goals. Watch out for "I don't know. Just lucky, I guess." And absolutely dismiss any applicant who replies, "Look, I'm out of bed and dressed. What more do you want?"

"Describe a situation when a customer left unhappy." You want signs that the candidate can accept responsibility for a negative situation.

"Why did you decide to leave your present (or previous) position?" The candidate's answer will tell you what truly motivates them: more challenge, more money, more recognition or more prestige.

TIP Pest Control

"What kind of people irritate you most?" The candidate's answer to this question is like a mirror into the soul because his or her personality, most likely, is the direct opposite of the type he or she describes. It's a trick question, really, because candidates for server positions will feel compelled to answer "I'm a people person. I get along with everyone" to give you the impression that they'll be able to deal with any type of customer. Asking this question helps to establish how the applicant will work in a team environment. So the true go-getter personalities will answer something more like: "Lazy, negative complainers."

25 Server Types

Behavior-based questions for server candidates

Waiting tables effectively is a difficult job, certainly harder than it looks. So you shouldn't hire just *anyone* for server positions. The servers are the people who have the most direct contact with your customers — and the biggest impact on your business. Watch out for order-takers: walking, talking vending machines who act as if customers are an interruption of their job rather than the reason they have a job.

> **"If you hire a duck and then train a duck — all you've got is a trained duck."**
>
> —*Jill Livingston, Director of Training, VICORP*

Great servers are far more than order-takers. They are charismatic, personable *salespeople* who are comfortable being "on stage" in the dining room. They provide better service, sell more and smile more which keeps customers coming back ... with their friends.

If you want to hire people who'll go the extra mile for your customers, you need to go the extra mile to hire the best people available. That's why interviewing and hiring great front-line servers requires some different tactics than you'd use when hiring for other positions.

If you want to hire a server with suggestive selling skills, be sure to ask behavior-based questions that test those skills. For instance, *"Two customers order cheeseburgers and fries. What would you say to them?"* The correct answer would be something like, *"I would ask if they would like bacon or mushrooms on their burgers."* Now that's a salesperson!

Keep in mind, also, that great salespeople have highly competitive instincts that make them more responsive to sales incentives. So when interviewing and evaluating server candidates, watch for signs of a competitive spirit. To determine how self-motivated a candidate is, ask: *"Do you set goals for yourself?"* Follow up with: *"Tell me about one you set recently"* and *"What steps have you taken to achieve that goal?"* Also ask: *"What motivates you most?"* Is it money? Recognition? Rewards?

When interviewing applicants for server positions, appearance counts. You don't necessarily want to critique an applicant's choice of earrings, but you do want someone who is image-conscious during the hiring process — because that's an indication that they'll be conscious of your restaurant's image. Someone who comes to an interview in a ripped T-shirt and dirty jeans probably won't pay a lot of attention to the lasting images guests have of your restaurant. You'll also want to assess how skilled they are in providing good customer service. Ask: *"Can you describe a situation in your previous position when you had to deal with a customer who was upset with the service? How was it resolved?"*

Pencil Pushers

Another way to test a server candidate's suggestive selling skills is to make them prove their talents right there in the interview: Pick up any small object in the room (a pencil, watch, glass of water, etc.) and ask a server applicant to "sell" it to you. This little exercise will reveal a lot about the person's ability to sell, think fast and respond under pressure. Do they give up after your first objection — or do they continue selling until they seal the deal?

26 Note for Note

Note-taking tips for interviewers

Take notes. Some may tell you that note-taking during an interview is inhibiting to the candidate. Maybe, but consider the alternative. Research shows that shortly after hearing something, we forget most of it. Our retention rate a day later is only about 25 percent. Clearly, an applicant interviewed early has less of a chance than those interviewed later. Note-taking actually benefits the applicant because later your notes will help you to clearly differentiate one applicant from another. Without notes, you'll have to rely on a "gut" reaction, which isn't always the best judge of character.

And, with the legal ramifications associated with job interviewing these days, detailed note-taking is a must. On the other hand, "bad" notes are worse than no notes at all. Make sure periodically to review the notes of those conducting interviews to make sure they include pertinent information or if they suggest discriminatory intent or conclusions.

Usually what makes candidates uncomfortable with the process is watching their interviewer concentrating more on a notepad than on the conversation. Too often when interviewers take notes, they spend most of the time scribbling feverishly, only to find random words and snippets of important points when they review their notes later. Interviews go too quickly to try to write down every spoken word.

Some interviewers make the process doubly hard by trying to decide *during* the interview whether they're going to hire the applicant. Leave the analyzing for later. For now, just focus on recording key information. Your goal is to concentrate on active *listening* rather than active *writing*. Before the interview, review the application so you are familiar with the applicant's experience. That way you won't waste time during the interview re-writing information you already have.

Most important, try to concentrate on the motivations behind the words and write *those* down. It requires using both your conscious and subconscious minds to hear the information, process it, write it down and continue with the interview. Your conscious mind will be focused on writing while your subconscious mind is reacting and making connections. Eventually, with practice, you'll be able to combine what you learn through *both* sides of your mind for more concise notes.

Immediately after the interview, go back through your notes and fill in any information you may have omitted — even if you have another interviewee waiting. You won't want to confuse the two applicants.

TIP Note-Taking Tips for Interviewers

- Use your own form of shorthand — key words, not whole sentences.

- Use a clipboard so the applicant can't see what you're writing.

- Don't stop writing if you're surprised by something the applicant says.

- Do stop writing if the applicant's statements seem to demand your full attention.

- Maintain eye contact with the applicant as much as possible.

27 Form and Function

Create an interview form to keep things on track

If you've knocked yourself out trying to master the fine art of note-taking and you still end up with a page full of mystery scribbles, try creating an "Interview Worksheet." It's especially effective if you conduct a large number of interviews. And, if other managers interview applicants, the form will act as an outline so each applicant is interviewed in the same style. Later, when you make your decision, the standardized format makes it easier to weed out unsuitable candidates.

> "Few managers will deny that they are only as good as the people they hire. What is hard to believe is the haphazard way they actually go about filling openings."
>
> —*Jack Falvey*

The worksheet method works best if you can create the form on a word processor so that you can customize it for each position. At the top of the page, leave spaces to write in the applicant's name, the position he or she is interviewing for and the name of the interviewer. From there, create two columns: On the left, list interview questions and reminders to interviewers to explain certain restaurant policies. Title the right side of the page "applicant response."

Begin by writing interviewer instructions and sample scripts on the left side: *"Make small talk to put the applicant at ease. Tell the applicant your interviewing objectives: 'As you know, we're looking to hire a few new servers to join our team. I've looked through your application so I know a bit about your experience. What I want to learn now is a little more about your background and your personality. After that, we'll look through the job description and I'll answer any questions you have about us. I'll be taking some notes as we go so I'll be sure to remember you when we make our decision.'"* Then, write in general questions on the left side: *"How long have you lived here?" "Would you prefer full- or part-time?" "What days/shifts are you available to work?"*

Now you're ready for the tougher questions. Here's where you'll see the greatest benefit in using an interview worksheet. After all, you don't need to scribble out the applicant's answers word for word. All you'll need to recall later is whether the response was positive or negative in terms of fitting your needs. Begin by choosing a few questions from each category: Experience/skills, intelligence/aptitude and personality/attitude. On the right side of the page, type in a sample positive answer and a sample negative answer. Then, as you interview, simply circle "positive" or "negative" as the applicant responds. Leave a little extra space for notes in case the applicant says something that you'll want to recall. As you analyze candidates, look back through the right column for a one-page "image" of the candidate based on the number of positives, and make your decision.

Sample Interview Worksheet

As a member of the restaurant staff, how would you help develop repeat business?

Positive: Specifics that show personal action; e.g. "Learn and use guests' names."
"Make menu suggestions."
Negative: "Be friendly." "Be patient."

How do you feel about doing more than one thing at a time?

Positive: "I like it; it's a challenge."
Negative: "Doesn't bother me."
"Prefer to keep focused."

Is it difficult for you to carry on small talk with people you don't know?

Positive: "No, not at all."
Negative: "Sometimes."
"Depends on the situation."

(28) Hospitality Begins at the Interview

Put applicants at ease

Job interviews are stressful experiences for everyone. Think about it. Do you feel comfortable talking about yourself for half an hour to convince someone *you don't even know* that you're competent, intelligent and a good risk? Probably not. Contrary to popular belief, interviews need not be high-stress situations. In fact, you'll find out more about an applicant if you're able to put them at ease. As the interviewer, it's your responsibility to do everything you can to reduce a candidate's tension and establish a comfortable rapport.

Begin by treating applicants as first-class citizens. If you aren't the first person the candidate will see, let everyone on your staff know that you'll be interviewing candidates. Train them to say: "Hi, great to see you — we've been expecting you," instead of "Do you have an appointment?" Acknowledge the candidate quickly. Greet them with a smile.

Interview them as soon as possible — don't make them wait until you finish lunch or place an order with a supplier. If you positively can't avoid a delay, greet the candidate personally, apologize and give your best estimate of how long the wait will be. If it's going to be longer than 15 minutes, reschedule the interview.

Make applicants feel more comfortable. Be friendly, just as you would with a customer. Hold doors open. Hang up their coats. Offer them a cola or a cup of coffee. Never, ever make them pay for it! Make them feel wanted by being hospitable. Maintain eye contact, nod your head up and down, don't interrupt. And try not to act surprised by something an interviewee might say.

There are two very good reasons for going to all this effort. First, it's difficult to maintain a conversation with a candidate who is uncomfortable or nervous — and that means you're not getting the information you need to make an informed decision. Unless you can get the candidate to relax, you'll never get an accurate picture of the candidate. There is validity to the argument that if people can't handle the stress of a job interview, how will they handle the stress of the restaurant industry? But that's no excuse for intentionally treating people poorly. Which brings up reason number two: What if, even after a particularly unpleasant interview experience, the candidate maintains composure and turns out to be the best person for the job? You could have trouble convincing the applicant to accept the position if he or she feels mistreated.

TIP

Setting the Interview Scene

- **Remind your staff that you shouldn't be interrupted during interviews.**

- **Allow enough time for the interview and your own note-taking.**

- **Select a quiet area to hold the interview — preferably a table in the dining room where candidates will be more at ease than in your office across a desk.**

- **Put the applicant at ease; remember how you felt when you first interviewed for your job.**

29 Open Communication

Test applicants' communication skills

Make small talk during the interview. Not only will it help put the interviewee at ease, it will give you a good indication of how comfortable the candidate is communicating with others. Candidates for *all* your positions will need good communication skills. That goes, obviously, for servers, greeters or cashiers, but kitchen staff, too. How can you expect to build a team if you can't keep communication flowing within the team? People *have* to be able to talk in this business.

Begin every interview by asking questions that encourage a conversation. *"How are you today?"* just doesn't cut it because it'll prompt only a one-word answer. Avoid "yes" and "no" questions, as well, for the same reason. Try something more along the lines of *"Great shoes! Where'd you get those?"* or *"You look familiar — did you visit the restaurant recently?"* Use their answers to spark another question until you have a full-blown conversation going. It'll set the tone for the entire interview.

As you run through your list of serious questions, throw in a couple of fun ones to help ward off nervous tension. Fun questions don't have to be just tension relievers, though. Use them to get information you may not otherwise have uncovered. Ask server candidates: *"So, what was the name of the last movie you saw?"* Not only will it break the formality, but if their answer is a current release, you can usually guess that they're pretty social in their private lives. People who are more social make better servers — and have an easier time making small talk with customers.

Ask: *"What's the most embarrassing thing that's ever happened to you?"* You're not necessarily interested in the answer. You'll want to watch for their reaction and their body language. Does their brow furrow as they look away nervously, or are they able to laugh and look you in the eye while explaining a less-than-flattering story about themselves? A sense of humor is mandatory in the restaurant business.

TIP   Solitary Man

If you come across applicants that seem uncomfortable with this type of "idle chitchat", ask a few questions regarding how well they communicate. For instance, "How important was communication and interaction with others in your last job? You may discover that a prep cook or dishwasher candidate was isolated from the rest of the staff and never had to communicate with anyone. If your operation thrives on regular communication among staffers, a person who prefers isolation may not excel. Also ask: "What other members of the staff were you required to interact with? Did you encounter any difficulties?" He may tell you that he only had to deal with kitchen staffers on his last job. You may even find out that servers and buspeople "get on his nerves because they can be so demanding." If your operation requires regular interaction, he or she may not be a suitable candidate.

30) When You Assume...

Avoid interview stereotypes

Everyone has their own preconceptions about others. Judging people from first impressions is, after all, human nature. But in interviews and later when evaluating an applicant's potential, you must be honest enough with yourself to push those biases aside. They could make you turn away the best employee your restaurant has ever had — or convince you to hire someone you shouldn't.

For instance, just because someone's young doesn't mean they're immature or irresponsible. Besides, if you automatically rule out younger people, you've alienated the generation that makes up much of today's foodservice work force. Conversely, don't assume that just because someone's older they'll show up for work on time every day. Don't reject an older applicant because you don't think they'll fit in a "young" or "energetic" work environment.

Not all overweight people are lazy. Not all short people have Napoleon complexes. Not all blondes have a low intelligence quotient. An applicant who comes well dressed to the interview won't necessarily do a great job. That applicant may suit your notion of an ideal "image," but dress appearance alone is not a guarantee of good work performance. What about an applicant with a college degree? Do you automatically assume that academic credentials mean higher intelligence? On the flip side, do you hold a secret grudge against people with more education than you?

"You can't tell how far a frog can jump by just looking at it."

—*Moultre Hale Cornelius III, Texas-born restaurateur and sage*

How about people with disabilities? Can you look beyond the disability and hire them for what they *can* do? According to Title I of the Americans with Disabilities Act of 1990, it's against the law to discriminate on the basis of disability in *any* aspect of the employment process, including testing, hiring, promotions, compensation, benefits or termination. Any inquiry about whether a candidate has a disability or the severity of the disability is prohibited.

The important point to understand is that stereotyping can lead you astray when hiring. First impressions *do* have a certain validity, but you have to look beyond that initial opinion to discover who's on the inside. Fact is, you can never really predict how an interviewee will perform on the job — no matter what you see.

Law Breakers

Preconceptions can not only make you pass up otherwise qualified candidates, they may just win you a hefty lawsuit. Avoid questions on any of these topics:

Age (including whether a person over 40 will fit in a "young" environment)	**Convictions/arrests except as related to job functions such as cash handling**
Military (questions about discharge)	**Organizations, clubs and societies**
Citizenship	**Religion (including holidays observed)**
Disabilities	**Height/Weight**
Name (questions about its origin)	**Race or color**
National origin or birthplace	**Residence (relationships)**
Marital or family status	**Pregnancy and medical history**

69

31 Check This Out

Tips for checking references

Make checking references a priority. The cost in time and money is small compared to the cost of firing people later when you discover their true colors. Don't rely solely on a candidate's longevity at his or her last job. The former employer may have had much lower standards and a more lax atmosphere than what you may require.

Unfortunately, reference checking has become a legal mine field. Employers can be sued for giving bad references, or simply giving references the candidate doesn't like. The result: Many employers do nothing except confirm dates of employment. Some creative job seekers therefore assume that disinformation on applications will go undetected. That's why it's important to check. But before you begin, get the candidate's approval. On job applications, add a box asking applicants for the authority to check the references they list and make sure they sign it.

When calling to check a reference, tell the applicant's former manager or supervisor: *"We're thinking about hiring Dick Credenza. He gave me permission to contact you to verify a few facts about his employment with you. Of course, everything you tell me will be held in strictest confidence. Do you have a couple of minutes to talk?"* Here are some good (and legal) questions to ask:

"Would you say the applicant is more of a people-oriented person or a technically-oriented person?"

"You can't talk your way out of what you've behaved yourself into."

— A.J. Edelstein, Regional Director of Operations, Harborage I, Inc.

"Did the applicant typically assume responsibilities beyond the scope of the job description or did he or she adhere to a strict interpretation of duties?"

"How did the applicant relate to supervisors?"

"How did the applicant adapt to new situations?"

Tell them the position the applicant is applying for and record any reactions they have. Confirm that the applicant held the position listed on the application, as well as the name of the last supervisor, dates he or she was employed, rate of pay and the reason for leaving.

And one of the best — and most telling — questions you can ask is: *"Would you re-hire this person?"* If you receive no other information from a reference check, this answer will be your best judge of the applicant's capabilities.

TIP

Tips On Checking References

- **Personally check references of candidates — don't leave it to someone else.**
- **Don't delay. Begin checking as soon as you get the candidate's permission.**
- **Pay little attention to written references a candidate supplies — of course they'll be favorable.**
- **Pay little attention to personal references for the same reason. Rely more on past employers, since they know the applicant's work style.**
- **Seek out references that were not provided by the candidate, and get as many as possible.**

32 Break the Rules

Hiring inexperienced candidates

As you analyze candidates, keep an open mind. Why not take a chance on a candidate who lacks the experience you were seeking? It's an age-old Catch-22: You can't get a job without experience and you can't get experience unless someone gives you a job. If a candidate for a server position has less-than-impressive career highlights, but demonstrates a real "showbiz" personality and a burning desire to work in your restaurant, that person may, in fact, be the right choice.

Have *you* ever applied for a job that you knew you weren't 100 percent qualified for — but you just *knew* you could do it? Most everyone has. Candidates who lack experience yet show a willingness to work hard to learn often turn out to be better employees than veteran know-it-alls. Plus, that applicant may bring a fresh perspective to your operation that you wouldn't otherwise have.

But that's not to say you should throw caution to the wind when an inexperienced candidate walks through the door. You'll simply need to modify your line of questioning. Even if an applicant hasn't waited tables before, he or she has certainly *dined* at a restaurant before. Who hasn't? Instead of basing the interview on restaurant work history, ask the potential employee to detail good and bad experiences he or she has had as a restaurant *customer*. Find out if the applicant has strong feelings about receiving good customer service. How does the applicant define the customer-employee relationship? You'll also want to ask if

> "The person at the top of the mountain didn't fall there."
>
> —*Tom Lackmann,*
> *Lackmann Foodservices*

the applicant has dined at your restaurant. How would he or she rate the service received? What improvements would he or she make if hired?

On the other hand, don't eliminate a candidate from contention if he or she seems overqualified. Restaurant employees can be fickle about where they work — especially servers, because they can control the amount of tips they make so base salary isn't the biggest draw. Many will jump from one restaurant to another looking for a place where they fit in best. Treat them well and they may just stay with you longer than the average employee.

You may also encounter veteran servers who've moved on to other industries but wind up one day "between jobs." They may need to fall back on their serving abilities until something comes up in their field. Sure, they'll probably leave you when they find something — but who knows how long that could be? And if you treat them well and reward them for their efforts, they may just decide on a career change.

Job Hoppers

Don't automatically eliminate a candidate who's switched jobs frequently over the past couple of years. If you're looking for a server with polished suggestive selling skills, think about it this way: Anyone who can repeatedly sell him or herself at a job interview obviously has good potential as a salesperson. The candidate is clearly comfortable jumping through hoops to impress people. So it's reasonable to assume the candidate would handle your customers the same way. Delve into the job-jumping to find out the reasons why. Sure, excessive jumping could indicate instability, but if the candidate has bettered him- or herself with each change, you can usually assume a fairly high level of competence.

33 Second Opinions

Involve all of your staff in interviewing candidates

Every candidate you interview will present their most charming smile and likable manner — interviews automatically put people on their best behavior. But be on the lookout for people who are great at performing for interviewers, but lack the skills to do the job. Worse, maybe they aren't all they say they are. A great act can cover up incompetence and fool you into hiring the wrong person. It may be months before you discover that the employee is buttering up the boss while alienating his or her co-workers — and *even worse*, your guests. Think of the business lost!

How do these mistakes happen? Usually when the hiring decision is made by just one manager alone. Something about an applicant can win you over — a feigned enthusiasm, a counterfeit interest in your words and plans.

One way to guard against your own misjudgments is to enlist the help of other managers and key staff members. Have each applicant come in for second and third interviews, each conducted by a different manager. Coach your managers on interviewing techniques. They may pick up on something you missed about an applicant.

Create new lists of questions for follow-up interviews — make sure they get gradually more difficult. You may also consider instituting a series of tests for each of your positions. Why not make applicants *prove* they can do the job?

Another good way to avoid hiring mistakes is to solicit "second opinions" from the rest of your staff. For instance,

> **"It is wise to remember that you are one of those people who can be fooled some of the time."**
> —*Paul Beninati*

when that applicant came in to fill out an application, how did he or she treat your greeter? Make it a part of the interview process to take applicants on a tour of the restaurant. Introduce them to as many employees as possible — and give them the chance to chat.

Coach employees beforehand on "conversational" questions they should ask. Create a form to pass out to every employee who meets the applicant. It doesn't have to be anything fancy, just ask if the candidate was pleasant, respectful and, "Was this someone *you* would want to work with?" Don't base your final decision on any one employee's opinion. Rather, take them *all* into consideration. If the picture the applicant presents differs from your own, you may want to investigate a little further.

Red Alert

Be alert to these red flags when evaluating applicants:

- **Left previous job without adequate notice**
- **Late for the interview**
- **No verifiable references**
- **Must travel too far to work**
- **Angry about previous employment**
- **Has never dined at your restaurant**
- **Arrives at interview in inappropriate attire**
- **Bad-mouths former employers**

34 Final Analysis

Tips on making that final decision

The only problem with going through all the extra effort to successfully recruit quality applicants and improve your interviewing skills is that the final decision becomes much more *difficult* than it used to be. You'll have a large amount of detailed information on *only* those applicants good enough to make it through advanced screening. You and other members of your staff interviewed applicants, delving deep into their background, identifying personality traits and testing their skills. And you've carefully checked references with their former employers for additional opinions — this time from those who personally know the applicant's work habits.

The good news is, every applicant who makes it this far into the process and remains a top contender will probably make a suitable choice. But after all the trouble you've gone through to get to this point, don't give up and simply go with your gut instincts. The following steps will help when you enter the final analysis to ensure the *best* choice.

Limit the number of decision makers. Sure you should try to get the opinions of as many of your staffers as possible. But when it comes down to the final decision, do it yourself. You won't want to end up hiring a "compromise" candidate — one who meets the lowest common denominator.

Gather all your information together one last time. Read the job description and personality profile again, then read each candidate's application and interview notes or worksheet. Ask yourself: *"How would I feel if this person worked for my competition?"* If your answer is *"I really don't care,"* you'll be able to put that application in the "No" pile.

Once you've narrowed it down to two or three candidates, try to put yourself in *their* shoes. Will the position meet their criteria for an ideal job, based on what they told you in the interview? What's the likelihood that the hire will stick around? Try to picture each candidate on the job. See if you can visualize the person performing the regular functions of the job — particularly the more difficult aspects. One candidate may stand out over the others. If you still can't decide, ask yourself which applicant seemed to *want* the job the most. After everything else, this can often be the deciding factor.

Starting Over

What if you get all the way through the recruiting and interviewing steps and you don't feel strongly about *any* of the contenders? Never settle on the best of the worst! This is your chance to evaluate where you went wrong. For whatever reason, you were unable to attract the best applicants to your restaurant. This is your cue to go back to the recruiting process. Was there another source you overlooked that would have brought you a better response? Give it a shot before hiring a less-than-suitable candidate. It's frustrating, but you'll be better off in the long run. It's better to be understaffed for two weeks than to hire someone you know won't work out.

35 Mystery Applicants

Testing the skills of other interviewers

So you think you've got this hiring thing down. You've read all the books. You're recruiting in all the right places. You know how to ask the right questions. But still those less-than-suitable employees keep slipping through to muddle up your operation. What's gone wrong? Maybe you've prepared yourself to hire the best people, but other managers within your operation are still going with the same old "hire 'em if they can breathe" method that's so prevalent in the restaurant industry.

Hiring the best should be first and foremost on everyone's mind for the good of your operation. So train your managers with the best techniques for recruiting and interviewing quality employees. Then, test their skills by hiring "Mystery Applicants" to help you see where the problems are.

You're probably familiar with the idea of a "Mystery Shopper" program to evaluate customer service. A "Mystery Applicant" is basically the same idea. Setting up interviewees to evaluate the interviewing skills of other managers will help you identify the weak spots in your operation's hiring chain. Shifty? Well, maybe ... but keep in mind that you're evaluating interviewers to identify where there's a need for further *training* — not to get someone in trouble. And, by all means, *tell* your hirers that you may eventually send a Mystery Applicant their way just to see that they've retained and are using their training. That in itself may spur improvements.

> "We are hiring people to work for us who we wouldn't let in the front door as customers a year ago. What's worse, just try to find someone who is competent and passionate enough to manage those people."
>
> —*Vice president of a major restaurant chain who prefers to remain anonymous*

Begin by soliciting the help of people about the same age and personality type as your typical employee. Consider contacting a temporary agency — be sure to describe in detail what you're trying to do! Some restaurateurs have even contacted talent agencies for Mystery Applicants — aspiring actors will obviously be great at pretending to be someone they're not!

Explain your interviewing and hiring policies and philosophies so they know how they *should* be treated. You don't necessarily have to find people with restaurant experience. In fact, tell them to say they do anyway. If experience is one of your criteria and the interviewer can't see through the fib and recommends hiring the applicant, they obviously need some additional hiring training.

TIP

A View of the Interview

Use the following questions to create a form for Mystery Applicants to fill out afterward:

- Was the interviewer able to avoid interruptions?
- Did the interviewer make special efforts to put you at ease?
- Did the interviewer maintain eye contact?
- Did the interviewer take notes?
- Who did most of the talking?
- Did the interviewer review the job description and answer your questions?
- What aspects of the interview could have been handled differently?
- What questions were you asked?
- Did the interviewer ask any questions that are against the law?

III

"When someone leaves, it messes up your employee teams, messes up your productivity, and messes up the service you provide to your guests."

—*Richard Bell-Irving, Vice President of Human Resources Division, Marriott Hotels, Resorts and Suites*

CHAPTER THREE:
Keeping the Best

Introduction

It's not a labor crisis — it's a *turnover* crisis. Too many managers concentrate their energies on finding and hiring good people, but blow the most important part: If those new hires leave you, you're back to square one. But if you can entice good employees to stay, you won't have to worry about recruiting and interviewing anymore.

Studies have shown over and over again that people leave most often because they are under-appreciated and under-trained. The 17 great ideas that follow will help you create an environment where employees will want to stay — an atmosphere of mutual respect where people are treated fairly and recognized for their contribution to the success of the operation.

You benefit as much as your employees do since creating a more comfortable and friendly atmosphere also helps attract more guests. How you treat your staff determines how they'll treat your customers.

Let's be honest. There's a hidden agenda in treating your staff well: Recruiting, hiring and training a new employee costs a great deal of money. It's an investment in the future of your operation. If these "investments" jump over to the competition, your loss becomes another restaurant's gain.

36 Great Beginnings

Effective employee orientations

Make every employee's first 30 days count! One of the best ways to retain great employees is to make them feel welcome and needed from their very first day. After all, this initial period is when they're forming the behaviors and attitudes they'll carry through their entire employment at your restaurant. Begin training them the minute they walk in the door and be sure the training is effective — you'll never have a better chance to teach them right.

New employees will all be a bit nervous on their first day, so be sure that you and your trainers make every effort to put them at ease. If you've hired several people for new positions, have them go through at least part of their orientation together in a group — even if they're training for different positions. There's strength in numbers! They'll develop camaraderie with their new teammates and gain a clearer understanding of their role as they learn about other positions.

As soon as possible, explain to new hires the importance of their individual positions as well as where they fit into the "big picture." Your enthusiasm at this point will raise interest in their new jobs.

Set high standards when training. You can't expect new employees to do a first-class job after seeing a second-class demonstration. As you train, make new employees feel free to ask questions. If they're not asking questions, that could be your cue that they're not understanding what you're teaching them. Give reasons for methods and pro-

'When one is helping another, both are strong.'
—*German proverb*

"An employee is never more focused, malleable, and teachable than the first day on the job."
—*Horst Schulze, CEO, Ritz-Carlton Hotels*

cedures in layman's terms — this applies to both the "telling" and the "showing" part of training. Your new employees will learn more easily and remember longer if they can attach meaning to the tasks. Teach skills that can be performed immediately, so your hires can feel productive on their first day.

Avoid criticism. Instead, show new employees "a better way" to do their tasks. Your praise and encouragement will help build their self-confidence. And be sure to follow up, checking each trainee's performance as often as possible.

Assign a Shepherd

Offer trainers a bonus after 30 or 60 days if the new employee they trained stays with the restaurant at least a month and has above-average performance over that time period. Why? The bonus helps the trainer "shepherd" the trainee into better skills over the first month of employment, and provides incentive to perfect teaching skills. Have the shepherd review the new hire's progress weekly to ensure that skills are improving. When you get employees involved in the teaching, you automatically get them involved in the learning. When you teach, you learn twice.

37 No Train, No Gain

Treat training as an ongoing process, not an event

Every successful restaurant manager knows that the training process doesn't end after the employee learns the initial functions of the job. At great restaurants, training is a philosophy, not a department. A well-trained staff not only helps you acquire and maintain more customers, it helps you acquire and maintain better employees. Better-trained servers make more money and provide better service to your guests. Better-trained kitchen employees get the job done more quickly and efficiently — and are happier with their jobs.

Your employees are your most important resource. Recognize them by training and re-training them monthly, daily — even hourly, customizing your approach to suit every greeter, server, bartender, busperson, cook and dishwasher. Make it your personal goal to teach everyone on your staff something new every day.

Base your training and performance evaluations on the behavior you expect, not just "attitude." You can have the best attitude in the world, but if your behavior doesn't change, there's no improvement. People can't repeat an attitude, but they can repeat behavior. They say it takes 21 days of different behavior to change a bad habit. That's why training *daily* is critical to eliminating "Teflon training" (training that just won't stick).

Keep in mind that it's not what's poured into a trainee that counts. It's what's planted. Nothing lasts as long as a box of cereal you don't like and a training session you can't stand. Make your training fun, lively and relevant.

The best place to begin is in daily pre-shift team meetings. They'll become the most important five or 10 minutes of the day for you and your staff. The brief format will allow you to give your staff something new to learn every day, set daily service and sales goals and fire up your staff to go the extra mile when serving guests.

TIP

Shift Into Gear

Tips for holding effective pre-shift team meetings:

- Keep it short and sweet — five or 10 minutes per day.

- Think dialogue, not monologue. Verbally quiz employees on product knowledge, daily specials and upcoming events or promotions.

- Conduct brief role-playing scenarios so servers can practice new techniques.

- Set daily sales goals and introduce incentives for servers and bartenders.

- Don't leave out the kitchen crew! Have a brief kitchen team meeting every day. Teach staffers about cost control, speeding up ticket times and ensuring quality. Then set incentives for them, as well.

- Use fun visual aids like flip charts, videos and workbooks.

38 Positive Feedback

Effective performance evaluations

Your employees will rarely perform *above* your expectations. That's why you should keep raising them. Constant feedback will show your employees where they stand — and where they should be going. Regular employee performance reviews are great tools for communicating your expectations, setting goals and celebrating when goals have been achieved. Here are some tips on conducting effective employee reviews.

Before the review, have employees do self-evaluations. It's a great way for you to gain a clear vision of their perception of their own strengths and weaknesses. It will help you and employees work together to identify those areas that need improvement.

During the review, evaluate each employee's performance based on the last period's goals. If those goals have been achieved, congratulations are in order!

Spend approximately 25 percent of the review discussing past performance, 15 percent on the present and 60 percent on outlining your expectations for the future. Concentrate on maintaining a *dialogue* with the employee. Don't lecture. Talk about his or her plans for the future. Is he or she interested in staying in the restaurant industry? Interested in training for any other positions within your operation? Work with the employee to prepare an "action plan" that outlines goals for the next period and the steps needed to achieve those goals.

> "Research shows time and time again that what employees want most is for their manager to tell them face to face they're doing a good job. Unfortunately, they most often hear from the boss when they've made a mistake."
>
> —*Bob Nelson, author*

Avoid evaluating personal characteristics and traits. Base your evaluation only on documented evidence of performance. Try not to be unfairly rough on an employee. But at the same time, don't be unduly easy. Be honest. The feedback you give the people who report to you has to reflect reality. Everyone knows you do a disservice to a B student when you award an A+. If you tell someone they're doing a perfect job, you're telling them they don't need to improve. Who can't benefit from improvement?

Make these reviews as regular as clockwork — every 30, 60 or 90 days, for instance. And follow up daily, so the employee knows if he or she is on the right track. Some managers make it a point to give employees "mini-evaluations" at the end of each shift. Providing feedback daily brings constant improvement.

TIP

Constructive Criticism

If you're bending the rules for one low-performing employee, the rest of your staff will certainly notice. Low standards produce low morale and low performance levels throughout your operation. That's why you can't be afraid to discipline when you see a problem. Here are some tips on doing it effectively:

- Discipline immediately
- Be specific in explaining the problem
- Focus on the performance problem, not the employee
- Ask for the employee's help in solving the problem
- Reach an agreement and write it down
- Express confidence in the employee's ability to solve the problem
- Praise the employee at the first sign of improvement

39 Love 'Em and Lead 'Em

Be a leader, not a boss

When your employees see you coming, do they say, "Here comes help!" or "Here comes trouble!"? When a dishwasher doesn't show up for his shift, are you screaming at the other dishwashers to pick up the pace, or are you dipping your hands in to get the job done?

You set the work atmosphere as manager and leader — and your employees will follow that lead. Are you thanking them for their dedication, praising them for accomplishments and having tolerance for honest mistakes? If you treat your employees with hostility and indifference, how will they treat your customers?

People want to succeed. Nobody comes to work to fail. It seems obvious — so why do so many managers operate on the principle that if people aren't watched and supervised, they'll bungle the job? Once you have the right people in place, you shouldn't have to worry about them getting the job done. Trust them to do their job just as you are trusted to do yours.

Give them your time. Realize that your dishwasher's request for five minutes of your time to discuss his schedule is as important as your boss' request for five minutes to discuss an upcoming promotion. After all, if both the dishwasher and your boss are supposed to show up for Friday's lunch and neither does, which one are you going to miss more?

"If you hire talented people and treat them badly, they'll screw things up for you. They'll slow you down and be rude to customers. Talented people don't necessarily do better unless you manage them well."

—*Donald Clifton,*
Chairman, The Gallup
Organization

Lay out concepts and ideas, but let your people execute them. Step back and allow them to *own* their work. Communicate your vision of an ideal restaurant to your staff. Be sure everyone understands it. Above all, truly appreciate your employees. They can make you or break you.

TIP

Open Communication

Open your mind before opening your mouth. Would *you* want to be spoken to the way you speak to your employees? Where do your communication skills fit into the chart below?

"Clock in; we need you."	"Hi, I'm glad you're here. We need some help. Can you clock in right away?"
"You're late. Where've you been?"	"I'm glad you're here. Is everything OK?"
"You're doing that wrong."	"Here's a way that might work better."
"Clock out; it's slow."	"Who'd like to go home early today?"
"If you don't like it, look for another job."	"Please, it's busy and we need you. When it slows down we'll talk about this."
The silent treatment	"You made the difference. Thank you!"

40 Fair Play

Be consistent on policies, procedures and scheduling

How would you feel if you were always asked to work holidays or the closing shift while the manager's "favorites" seemed to be scheduled for only the choice shifts? Wouldn't *you* hate coming to work if every day you had to watch as your supervisor chats and jokes with a few favored employees, but then growls, "Get back to work" when he passes you? Be consistent on policies, procedures and communication. Employees want to be treated equally. Showing favor to only part of the staff will create resentment throughout.

Make it a point to greet each and every employee *by name* every day. Hold a personal conversation with each of them. "Work the room" of your *internal* customers just as you would with your guests.

And be fair when it comes to scheduling and discipline. Don't bend the rules for anyone no matter what the circumstances — and don't leave discipline to the whim of a supervisor. One of the best ways to avoid any unnecessary conflicts is to make every staff member aware of his or her own responsibilities as they relate to the whole operation.

If your operation doesn't already have a written personnel policy or employee handbook, you may want to create one. In it, include your restaurant's policies on scheduling, sick leave, vacation, overtime, paychecks, meal discounts, incentives and an organization chart. It will show employees that they're the most important asset of your business.

> "You can take great people, highly trained and motivated, and put them in a lousy system and the system will win every time."
>
> —*Geary Rummler, President, The Rummler-Bache Group*

Be careful, however, that your handbook does not become a "contract" or create additional obligations to "treat employees fairly" that restrict your flexibility to terminate or discipline employees. Your employee handbook should contain a conspicuous disclaimer that the handbook does not create a contract with the employee and the employer reserves the right to change conditions unilaterally and without notice.

Avoid making promises to "treat everyone fairly" or language specifying detailed termination procedures. It is a good idea to run the handbook by legal counsel to make sure it doesn't create problems.

Give a copy to each new hire. When you update it, make sure you pass out new copies that contain language that the new handbook replaces the old handbook so everyone on staff is always on the same page.

A Helping Handbook

Most operators complain that their handbooks are too long, too tedious and too packed with legal mumbo-jumbo. Here are some tips to help you build a better handbook:

- **Begin with the restaurant's history, including amusing service anecdotes. It will make employees feel like primary characters in an ongoing epic.**
- **Include a "mission statement" outlining your operation's philosophy, and refer to it as you explain policies. It tells the "why" along with the "how."**
- **Make the tone of the writing more welcoming than authoritative. Use shorter sentences and smaller words. Use bulleted lists rather than long paragraphs. Add lively illustrations to entertain the reader's eye.**
- **Make it user-friendly with a table of contents, a question and answer section, an index and cross-referencing.**

41 Power to the People

Empowering employees to solve their own problems

If guests have problems with their meal or with their service, do you encourage your servers to run and look for a manager for help — or to solve the problems on their own? Once you've hired good people, trust them to make decisions and solve problems.

First, train your front-of-the-house staff in the proper techniques for handling customer complaints. And let them know that you will back up any action they take to please the guest. Allow them to take matters into their own hands to solve customer problems — whether it means comping menu items, making substitutions or making other amends to satisfy the customer. Empowering your employees to solve problems not only encourages them to take more responsibility for their guests' dining experiences, it also sends a powerful message to your guests — it says that you have full faith in the people who will be providing their service.

Involve your employees in the decision making for your entire operation. The best way to get employees past a problem is to get them involved in the solution. If you have a problem with poor service, soaring costs or low sales, present the challenges to your staff. Break them into teams and ask *smart* questions, like *"What can we change to improve our service, lower our costs and increase our sales?"* or *"What are some of the reasons we're experiencing these problems now?"* People don't argue with their own data. Encourage them to brainstorm as many solu-

> **"Empowerment is the recognition that employees are not as dumb as employers thought they were."**
> —*Darryl Hartley-Leonard, President, Hyatt Hotels Corp.*

tions as possible in 15 minutes. Award the team generating the most ideas with individual one-dollar lotto "quick-picks" for their "million-dollar" contributions.

Try delegating more of your management duties to your employees. It will free you up to do more, create variety for those who report to you and develop a more responsible team. Another way to empower employees is to let everyone have a part in training. If you have a particular server who's excelling in suggestive selling, let her lead a training session on the subject. Getting your employees involved in training will encourage them to share their strengths, and it will keep their jobs from becoming mundane.

TIP

Take It to the Board

Form an "Employee Board" of five or six employees from all departments in the restaurant. Assign as their first task assessing employee satisfaction. Are they happy with their jobs? Do they know how they fit into the organization in terms of its goals and objectives? The group should be headed by an executive officer, and no direct supervisors should be present, so that the employees can speak freely. The Employee Board will also be a great means for gathering facts from employees regarding problem areas in the restaurant, or concerns they have with their work environment. Give the Board fun tasks, too, like testing new menu items, planning staff outings, etc.

42 It's Who You Know

Know their names, find out everyone's dream

Too many managers still go by averages. They talk about "our kitchen crew." When what they really have is Marcela, John, Penny, José and Steve. Each member of that kitchen crew is a different individual, a different personality — and deserves to be treated as such. You can no longer manage a work force. You must manage individuals.

Know their names. You sound silly if you don't. Everyone wants to feel as if they're an integral part of the team — but if you were greeted with "Hey, you — go fill up waters on table five," would you want to come to work every day? And what impression would that dialogue leave on a customer who happens to overhear it? Make it a point to greet every member of your staff — by name — every day.

But even that's not enough to build a positive work environment. How well do you really know your people? What's your cashier's boyfriend's name? Are they getting married anytime soon? Your dishwasher's about to graduate from college — now what was his major? Too often, managers ask a lot of questions during job interviews, but never bother to speak to the employee again unless it's to bark out an order.

Find out everyone's dream. Get to know your people. Where do they want to go? What do they want to be? You may be surprised who you'll meet: An aspiring actress. A future psychologist. If you take the time to get to know your busperson, you may discover that he's interested in

> "Know your people, know their strengths. Know your work and its requirements. Bring them into closer alignment. It seems terribly obvious."
>
> —Ned Herrmann, founder of the Ned Herrmann Group and former head of management training for General Electric Co.

becoming a restaurant manager. Share what you know with him and he could be your next management trainee.

Celebrate victories publicly. Your employees aren't just walking, talking robots, and they don't necessarily live and breathe for the good of your restaurant. They have goals and dreams outside of work that are important to them. When big things happen in their lives outside the restaurant, that's cause for a celebration. Host a graduation party for that dishwasher. It doesn't have to be anything formal, just recognize the accomplishment. Your cashier just got engaged and your cook's wife just had a baby — these are major life events! Make them celebrations for everyone on your staff.

Social Hour

If you don't know your employees well, chances are they don't know each other well, and they're probably not working together as a team. The solution? Throw a staff party where employees can socialize, chatting about themselves and their interests. Create a "Staff Yearbook" form. On it, ask personal questions about their favorite music, the last movie they've seen, their dream job, the names of their pets, their "ideal" weekend, etc. While crew members mingle, have each fill out a form. You and other managers should fill one out, too. Take Polaroid pictures of everyone and attach them to the questionnaires. Hang the pages around the restaurant for staff to read. Later, compile the forms and Polaroids into a "yearbook" binder. As you hire new people, show them the yearbook to help them get acquainted with co-workers — and have them fill out their own questionnaire during their training.

43 Field of Dreams

Let students test their skills by helping you with management tasks

Everyone on your staff has capabilities beyond their job description. Look around. Your bartender is a marketing major at the local university. Your dishwasher is studying to be a computer programmer. Your greeter wants to pursue a career in public relations. And your best server is a graphic artist who's "between jobs," making a living at your restaurant until something comes along in his field. Sure, these talented employees may eventually leave you to follow those dreams. But while you've got them, why not tap into their talents for the benefit of your operation?

Allow your employees to get involved in the day-to-day operation of your restaurant by assigning them tasks that apply to their chosen careers. Have your marketing major help plan your next promotion. Solicit the help of that graphic artist to design flyers and advertising for the event. Have that public relations student work on getting media coverage. Have a music major audition and hire bands for live performances.

By delegating these tasks to your employees, you'll save the money you would have spent on hiring an outside contractor — or you'll save yourself the time you would have spent doing them yourself, which gives you more time to concentrate on other management functions.

More important, you'll provide your employees with valuable hands-on experience they can put on their résumé when they decide to move on. It shows your employees

> 'One of the stepping stones to a world-class operation is to tap into the creative and intellectual power of each and every employee."
>
> —*Harold A. Poling, Chairman and CEO, Ford Motor Company*

that you support them in achieving their career goals, and respect them not just for who they are, but for who they want to be. You'll increase their sense of worth on the job — which translates into happier, more productive employees who won't jump to the competition.

Where Credit's Due

TIP

You can't have something for nothing — so you'll have to think about a way to compensate these employees for their expertise. Sure, you might find some who are just itching to try what they've only read about in textbooks. But, for the most part, employees will want a little something extra. Consider contacting the college to inquire about providing students with course credits for their contributions. The arrangement would develop into an internship and you'll get more dedication from your students since their work will be graded and figured into their GPA.

44 Fond Farewells

Hold exit interviews

> "You don't hire people, you rent behavior."
> —*W. Steven Braun*

Face it: You can't keep good people forever in the restaurant business. Sure, there are servers out there who began young and decided to make serving a career. But many people pass through the restaurant business on their way to other careers. And that's OK. Becoming a better recruiter, interviewer and leader will help you reduce hiring mistakes. But because of the nature of the business, you'll never be able to stop turnover completely.

When good employees decide to move on, don't take offense. Wish them well and try to view the turnover as a positive. It's an opportunity to learn from the experience and make changes accordingly. When possible, hold exit interviews with departing employees. It's a great way to find out what your employees *really* think about your operation and your management style.

Exit interviews should be just as organized as hiring interviews. You should create a format for all your managers to follow so they can conduct these interviews effectively. Trouble is, each exit interview will be slightly different depending on the individual's reason for leaving.

For example, if your best server has resigned after four years because she's graduated from college and has been offered a "real job," the exit interview should have a more casual tone. Your goal is to find out what attracted her to the job and what made her stay for so long. Ask things like, *"What did you like about working here?" "What didn't you like?"* (encourage her to be honest!) and *"Based on your four years here, what qualities and experience do you think your replacement should have?"* Her answers will tell you what you're doing right — things you'll want to continue doing to find and keep other good employees.

Exit interviews are particularly important when an employee leaves because he or she is unhappy with the work environment. Your goal is to find out the specific problems that are driving the employee away: Policies? Management? Co-workers? Rate of pay? If they're leaving to work for a competing restaurant, ask: *"What do they have to offer that we don't?"* Consider making a counter offer. But rarely will happy employees leave just for money or perks. Find out what they're unhappy about. Ask: *"How would you have handled this differently?"* Be sincere. Obviously the problem was big enough to send the employee someplace else — it deserves your full attention. Try to analyze the mistakes you may have made so you can avoid losing future employees.

Learning from Mistakes

TIP

When it's possible, hold exit interviews even when a person is fired. Respect the wishes of the employee who doesn't want to participate, but if the person agrees to it, first decide *who* will do the interview. The supervisor who called for the firing may not be the best choice. Have at least two interviewers in attendance, as exit interviews can be touchy on the legal side. Solicit the help of neutral staff members. Change your questioning (he or she may get hostile at *"What did you like about working here?"*). Instead, ask *"Why do you think it got to the point of termination?"* and *"If you had been the supervisor in this situation, what would you have done differently?"* A firing may not be the employee's fault. It could signal a weak link in your management chain. Something went wrong in hiring, training, performance appraisals or, possibly, your leadership was lacking. Make changes accordingly.

45 Cut Your Losses

Get rid of your bad employees

Weed out the trouble-makers, the loafers and the whiners in your operation to make room for more good employees. It's a harsh step — and you may ask if you can really *afford* to do something so drastic. Truth is, though, you really can't afford *not* to. You can't continue to let your restaurant's service suffer because you aren't sure if you'll be able to replace those employees. There's an easy solution: Become a better recruiter and interviewer. Pay more attention to the people you're hiring and you'll decrease your chances of having to fire anyone.

But that won't happen overnight and the hiring process will never be foolproof. A few stragglers will slip by and create a negative work environment for all your employees who are trying to do a good job. Negativity is contagious. As it spreads throughout your staff, morale drops lower and lower. And with it plunges your staff's productivity. That's no way to build teamwork. Surround your stars with more of the same and watch their positive vibes permeate the restaurant. Your *customers* will notice the difference.

But, before you go cleaning house, ask yourself what it is about a particular employee that's not working out. Attitude? Bad habits? Inability to do the work? Then ask yourself if there's something that can be done to correct the problems and avoid an emotional termination. Could that employee have been better trained? Confusion is the result of ineffective or nonexistent training. And confused people cannot act. Train first before you have to let them go.

> "If you can't change your people, then you *must* change your people."
>
> —Tom Hopkins, author, speaker

> "It's not what you pay a man but what he costs you that counts."
>
> —Will Rogers, quoted by Richard M. Ketchum, Will Rogers, His Life and Times, *1973*

Maintain an open dialogue with employees who are having trouble. Begin the process informally, giving employees the opportunity to change their behavior before pulling out the pink slips. When you meet with them, be clear and specific about the problems and about what changes you expect. Make the meetings and your record-keeping more formal if problems persist, but be careful not to "build a case" against a particular employee. Make sure your practices and records are consistent with similar behaviors of other employees.

Moving On

When it becomes clear that firing an employee is the only possible recourse, you owe it to that employee to act decisively. Firings are difficult, but not fatal. In time, as you perfect your hiring abilities, you will have fewer opportunities to perfect your firing abilities. But until then, here are a few tips to get you through termination meetings quickly and painlessly:

- Be as considerate as you can — think of how you would want to be treated.
- Make the meeting as brief as possible.
- Follow the necessary legal guidelines for firing, including reference to previous written warnings, non-performance of job requirements, etc.
- Do not review old sources of dispute — it will just cause a fight.
- Make it clear to the employee that it's too late for another chance.
- Talk about the person's performance, not personal characteristics or traits.

46 Bridging the Gap

Communicating with a younger generation

If you've ever caught yourself asking, "Why don't they just grow up?" about your younger employees, you've got a generation gap problem. No, they're not getting younger every year — you're getting older. And with this industry's fierce competition for employees, you have little choice but to hire young people. So you'd better learn how to work with them.

Your challenge in bridging the gap is to take the time to zero in on what makes them tick and what ticks them off. Run down the following list of turn-ons and turn-offs:

Turn-ons

Recognition and praise

Time spent with managers

Learning how what they're doing now is making them more marketable for the future

Opportunities to learn new things

Fun at work, structured play, harmless practical jokes, cartoons, light competition and surprises

Small, unexpected rewards for jobs well done

Turn-offs

Hearing about the past — especially yours

Inflexibility about time

Workaholism

Being watched and scrutinized

Feeling pressure to convert to traditionalist behavior

Disparaging comments about their generation's tastes and styles

Feeling disrespected

Source: Lawrence J. Bradford and Claire Raines

The key to keeping your young hourlies turned-on is training — and not the kind based on the outdated principles of boot camp. Like it or not, we're in the age of Sonic the Hedgehog and Beavis and Butt-Head, and your training should reflect that. What you need, as Beavis might say, is training that doesn't suck. If you're purchasing training programs off the shelf, look for ones that infuse a lot of fun into the mix and appeal to MTV sensibilities. What was good enough for Baby Boomer training 20 years ago *won't* work for Generation X.

The Perfect Guest Check

While there's still something to be said for a pat on the back for a job well done, you'll get more mileage out of incentives designed to motivate younger people. They'll always want to know "What's in it for me to improve service, increase sales or cut costs?" The better you answer those questions, the better you'll retain your young hourly employees. To fire up younger servers: Challenge them to create a Perfect Guest Check, which includes an appetizer, a beverage (not tap water), an entree with a purchased add-on or side item, a dessert, a coffee and an after-dinner drink. Each time a server turns in a Perfect Guest Check, award him or her a small prize like a lottery ticket, and enter the server's name into a drawing for a larger prize. At the end of a certain period (say, a week or a month) draw the winning server's name and award gift certificates from local stores or dinner for two at another restaurant.

47 Think Sales! Teach Sales!

Teach servers to sell

Train your servers and bartenders to think and act like salespeople. Why? Because they'll make a lot more money. Which, in turn, will make them happier employees. Hey, it really *does* buy happiness! Plus, your guests will receive better service since your waitstaff will be more in tune to their needs — which will keep those guests coming back. That's going to make your restaurant more profitable — which, in turn, will make you a happier manager, which will make you treat your employees better, which means happier employees who stay with the restaurant longer. Such is the cycle of success!

So where do you begin? Invest in waitstaff sales training programs that will teach your employees the art of suggestive selling. Tell your waitstaff that all they have to do is recommend products on the menu — and the worst that will happen is the guest may say "No." Emphasize the fact that all of those guests they serve every day have come in to the restaurant to buy something. If the server makes suggestions that convince the guest to buy more, hey, that means higher check averages and bigger tips. How much more? By increasing sales a mere $1 per guest, with an average of 50 guests per shift, servers will earn an extra $37.50 a week — or close to $2,000 more every year.

Besides, they'll learn how to work smarter, not harder — which means less time in "The Weeds" where even adequate service is impossible. With sales training, you'll be able to turn your "order-takers" into "service-oriented salespeople" who are able to guide guests through the menu, making suggestions and answering guests' questions. Servers will be able to control their sections, saving steps along the way, instead of letting their sections control them.

Higher Sales in Three Easy Steps

Teach your waitstaff these three steps and watch their check averages soar:

1. **Know your products. Memorize each menu item in terms of "The Four P's": portion, preparation, presentation and price.**

2. **Use your props. Table tents, menus, appetizer lists, dessert trays, bottles of wine, etc. Customers buy more when salespeople impact several senses while describing menu items.**

3. **Use the "Pencom Nod." It's a subtle use of body language that encourages guests to agree with menu suggestions. Simply smile and nod your head up and down while saying, "Would you like to try some guacamole on those nachos?"**

48 Eyes on the Prize

Creating effective staff incentives and contests

Understand that you cannot "motivate" anyone. All people *are* motivated, but they do things for their own reasons. You can rant and rave about increasing sales, improving service or lowering costs, but it won't mean a lot to your employees who are just trying to get through their shift with a few bucks in their pocket. You can, however, create an environment in which your employees are self-motivated. And one of the best ways to do that is with incentives and contests to improve performance. Which, in turn, improves your profits. So everyone gets what they want! Here are some tips on creating incentives and contests that get results:

Remember that it often takes a different approach to motivate each individual. What motivates servers won't motivate the kitchen crew. Arrange different incentives for every segment of your restaurant. Create an incentive to motivate the kitchen crew to control costs. Create another to encourage greeters to learn and use guests' names. And another to encourage buspeople to pick up the pace.

Start with the end in mind. Determine your specific desired result before you begin. Then plan and set goals backward. Communicate that goal to your staff in terms they'll understand. If, for instance, you want to increase appetizer sales by 10 percent this month, don't tell them, "To achieve this goal, we must sell 1,200 more appetizers this month." Break it down for them: "If we just sell 40 more appetizers per day, 20 per shift — that's only two per server,

> "The point of contest, incentive and recognition programs is that they make everyone feel that service and sales are his or her individual responsibility. That not only leads to better service for the customer, it also means higher morale for the staff."
>
> —*Lauren O'Connell, Citicorp*

per section, per shift. We can easily achieve this goal." It will inspire your staff to see how their individual efforts fit into the big picture.

Don't set quotas — work together to set goals. If you tell servers to sell 10 desserts on their next shift, that's *your* goal, not *theirs*. Employee "buy in" to your incentive or contest is critical to its success. They must agree not only on how to achieve the goal, but also what behavior is necessary to achieve the goal.

Post a contest board so everyone can see their progress. Reward those who achieve goals and re-train those who don't. Be creative in selecting prizes. Awards can include merchandise, gift certificates or simply praise in writing. Structure your incentives and contests so there will be several winners. For servers, reward not only the highest check averages or highest sales per hour, but also the most-improved sales percentage. It will eliminate the "same-server-always-wins" syndrome.

The Top 10 Ways to Reward Good Work

1. Prizes
2. Fun
3 Recognition
4. Money
5. A piece of the action

6. Advancement
7. Freedom
8. Personal growth
9. Time off
10. Favorite work

49 Instant Gratification

Daily contests, daily rewards

Sales contests are great tools for boosting morale while encouraging servers to try out new sales techniques. Great salespeople are very competitive, and they love contests because they like to win. But sometimes long sales contests get too tedious and servers give up halfway through.

Research has shown that contests and incentives for hourly workers get the best results when held, measured and rewarded within, *at a maximum*, a 28-day period. Employees tend to lose interest in a contest after a month, no matter how great the theme you've chosen or how well it's organized. So keep your contests short and simple.

Consider also setting up a new mini-contest every day. It will give servers something to look forward to on every shift, without the burnout of longer contests. Prizes don't have to be as big as, say, a brand-new car. They could be a simple Lotto "quick pick" or your restaurant's own "funny money" (play money employees can use for purchases at your restaurant). So the cost to the restaurant is negligible compared to the increase in check averages brought on by the servers' extra efforts.

Month-long contests are normally effective for only nine days — the first four of the month and the last five. To keep your contest interesting and interactive, consider offering small, daily rewards to employees who hit their daily goals, especially during the middle of the contest's run. Reinforce the goals of the contest or incentive program

"Motivation is something you have to create each day. What you did yesterday doesn't count today."

— *Bill Flock, President of Bill Flock & Associates*

every day with members of your staff, using the contest board as a tool to encourage them to do better today than yesterday.

If you want to use the same contest format again because you are pleased with the results, reintroduce it the very next month with a different twist — maybe featuring a different menu item — and present new rewards after 28 days.

TIP

Ante Up

If you don't think you have time for complex daily contests, try a round of Sales Poker. It's easy and it will keep your servers' morale high and the competitive spirit growing. All you'll need is a deck of poker cards and a prize. First, review your sales record to determine which product area needs a sales boost. Then announce the contest to your staff and name the type of poker you're going to play — five card draw, perhaps. Shuffle the deck and explain the rules of the game. Say the sales focus is appetizers. Tell servers and bartenders to draw a card for each appetizer they sell over a set minimum of, say, five. They can also trade one card for another draw, in hopes of improving their hand. The employee with the best hand at the end of the shift takes home the prize.

50 A Pat on the Back

Recognition for a job well done

How often have you heard: "No one appreciates what I do until I don't do it!"? There are so many ways to reward employees for consistently good behavior — and it's one of the easiest and least expensive ways to retain your best employees. Sales incentives work great for motivating servers to increase check averages, but those incentives cover only one segment of your staff.

Don't get so caught up in big sales contests that you forget to reward people for the little things. All most people want is some recognition and a simple pat on the back for their hard work. So when someone consistently does their job well, let him or her know you appreciate them. Here are some tips on rewarding employees for a job well done.

Be timely and specific. To be effective, recognition needs to happen fast. If you wait weeks or months to say "well done," you won't have motivated the employee to repeat the behavior. Keep a stash of lottery tickets or movie passes to hand out on the floor when you catch an employee providing great service. It's inexpensive, instantaneous and motivational.

Match the reward to the achievement. If an employee solves a major business problem that saves the restaurant thousands of dollars, the reward should be more substantial than a reward for someone who, as a favor, comes to work on his or her day off.

"With so many ways to reward people, you may ask, 'How do I decide how to reward each person?' The answer is simple: Ask them."

—*Michael LeBoeuf*

Match the reward to the person. Think about what matters most to the individual. Dollars don't necessarily count. Rather, be thoughtful and creative. Call a person into your office just to say "good job" — don't discuss any other issues. Or call your staff together to read aloud a customer letter of praise. When paychecks go out, write a note of recognition on the envelope to employees who've excelled over the pay period.

Award bronze, silver, gold and platinum pins along with a plaque and a gift for each year of service. Not only does it recognize an employee for his or her long-term contribution, it sends a message to new employees that says their co-workers are in this for the long haul. Start an "Employee of the Month" program in which good employees are nominated by their peers and rewarded with a cash prize, gift certificates or merchandise. Hold an annual drawing to select the "Employee of the Year," and award a much bigger prize.

And the Winner Is....

Once a year, hold your own Academy Awards ceremony, recognizing those who have served the best, sold the most, made the biggest improvements, smiled most often, had the best attendance, maintained the cleanest uniform, etc. Have fun with the ceremony and make it as simple or elaborate as you wish. Send out invitations inviting the employees to bring a guest. Plan a menu for the big event. Post a list of the categories where employees can see it and explain the criteria for being nominated for each award. Establish an employee committee to select the winners. Create a statuette resembling the real "Oscar" for each winner and award a prize or gag gift that reflects the category being recognized.

51 Hail to the Chef

Don't forget the kitchen crew

Good service isn't just the server's responsibility. It takes a concerted effort from everyone on the crew: The prep cook, the food expediter, the dishwasher and the cook are just as important in providing a great dining experience for your guests.

But all too often, it's the kitchen crew that's forgotten when it comes to training, incentives and rewards. It's no wonder the kitchen is the department that sees the most turnover industry-wide. The root of the problem lies in the long-held perception that kitchen positions are secondary to front-of-the-house positions, and that kitchen crew members are somehow less-skilled and more easily replaced. Any successful manager who values his cook will certainly challenge that opinion. To run your restaurant successfully, you'll want to keep that entire department intact by treating them well.

First, begin referring to your kitchen crew as the "Heart of the House," because they truly are the heart and soul of your operation. You can't possibly continue without them.

Cross-train members of your kitchen crew so they'll learn new skills and keep their jobs from becoming mundane. And, should your cook come down with the flu, you won't be wiped out for the shift since you'll be able to rotate your prep cook in to cover the orders.

Show kitchen staffers that you value them by including them in your incentives. Though it might be easier to reward servers for sales behaviors, heart-of-the-house employees should never be overlooked. There are hundreds of ways a restaurant can reward kitchen staff. Create incentives to encourage them to cut down on waste, crank out orders more quickly and control costs, to name just a few. Or, team up kitchen workers with front-room workers for team incentives. They'll root each other on, which will build a sense of teamwork and camaraderie throughout your restaurant.

Chef's Specials

Challenge each of your cooks to create one special dish per week. Encourage them to be cost-effective, but allow them to be imaginative. That way they'll put a lot of pride in the dishes they prepare. Run the contest for as many weeks as you have cooks, keeping track of whose special sold the most. If one special does exceptionally well, consider adding it to the menu — and give the cook the option of naming the new dish. Announce the winner after every cook has taken a turn. This could also be an ongoing contest, with the cooks and their specials scheduled in a rotation. Ask your cooks what kind of prize would please them the most (within reason, of course) and award it to the winner.

52 It *Is* a Real Job

Change the perception of "careers" in the industry

> "Two men were laying brick. The first was asked, 'What are you doing?' He answered, 'Laying some brick.' 'What are you working for?' He answered, 'Five dollars a day.' The second man was asked, 'What are you doing?' He answered, 'I am helping build a great cathedral.' Which man are you?"
>
> —*Charles Schwab*

Sometimes it may seem like the labor pool is shrinking, since it's so hard to find good employees who'll stick around. At the same time, an average of 42 new restaurants open every day in the United States — that's over 15,000 new restaurants this year. If you think you're having staffing trouble now, where will you be in three years? The labor force *isn't* shrinking. It's the labor force's perception of the restaurant industry as a "career" that has dropped. Rarely, if ever, does a kindergartner say, "I want to be a waiter or a line cook when I grow up." And too few of the people currently working in the industry intend on staying. Restaurants have become only a resting place for young people looking to move on to "real jobs."

Truth is, though, these *are* real jobs. In Europe, serving others in restaurants is considered an honorable job. Even in the U.S., the level of skill and the rate of pay of restaurant jobs are comparable to many 8-to-5 office jobs. In fact, servers and chefs at higher-end restaurants often earn far more than college grads working within their fields. What's missing is the pride in this industry. Restaurant positions are considered somehow less noble than positions elsewhere — no matter how much skill is required.

Indeed, almost anyone with a desire to learn can pick up the skills necessary to be a server, greeter, busperson, bartender, dishwasher or a cook. But skills aren't everything.

It takes a certain flair to excel in the restaurant business. And those who have it will do well to stay in the industry. Too many managers, though, have fallen into the philosophy that *anyone* can be taught to perform the functions of these jobs — that every member of their staff is easily replaced. By communicating that mind-set to the staff, you not only create a negative work environment, but also a negative image of the entire restaurant industry. People want to feel that their expertise is unique — that their presence is necessary to ensure the success of the restaurant. And it's up to you, the manager, to communicate that feeling of uniqueness to each and every employee. Treat them like professionals — because they are. This is a great business, full of fun times and great opportunities. Pass it on.

TIP   Career Building

Even if employees decide not to make a career out of their restaurant jobs, you should emphasize that the skills they use every day in a restaurant environment are easily transferred to other industries. Servers, for instance, learn suggestive selling skills that they can take with them to a sales position elsewhere. Merchandising the menu is similar to merchandising items in a department store. And as customer service becomes the number one draw with consumers, industries across the board will be looking for people with the skills to treat their customers well. Constantly remind your employees that every day they spend working in a restaurant, they're building their resumés with skills that are highly marketable in today's service-conscious business world.

Action Plan

To put these ideas to work for you most effectively, we suggest following these steps:

- Read this book cover to cover.
- Take notes and make a list of the ideas from each chapter that best apply to your operation.
- Give a copy of this book to all of your managers, assistant managers, trainers and recruiters.
- Have them take notes and make lists of the ideas from each chapter that best apply to your operation.
- Schedule a meeting to discuss your operation's recruiting and hiring policies and procedures.
- Prioritize the lists of ideas to develop a "Recruiting Strategy," an "Interviewing and Hiring Strategy" and a "Managing for Retention Strategy."
- Assign a specific staffer to captain the implementation of each Strategy.

> "If you wait until something is broken to fix it, there may not be anything left to fix."
> —*John E. Martin, President & CEO, Taco Bell Corp.*

Recruiting Strategy

- Develop personality profiles for all positions.
- Research and identify other vehicles for placing classified ads: community newspapers, trade magazines, the Internet, etc.; prepare creative advertisements so they're ready when positions open.
- Research and identify alternative recruiting opportunities: college career services offices, high school career fairs, government agencies, trade shows.

- Develop and implement a "promote-from-within" policy and communicate application submission guidelines to staff.
- Develop and implement job-sharing, flex-time and buddy system scheduling policies.
- Review benefits packages offered to new hires.
- Schedule an all-staff meeting to discuss the operation's recruiting challenges and to announce "bounty" incentives for staff referrals.

Interviewing and Hiring Strategy

- Develop job descriptions for all positions.
- Review application forms and make any necessary revisions.
- Create a list of interview questions for each positions, incorporating an equal number of questions from each category: Experience/skills, intelligence/aptitude and personality/attitude and behavior-based questions.
- Create a standard interview form.
- Schedule an "interviewing skills" training seminar for all managers; discuss your operation's interviewing policies and procedures; train managers on effective note-taking skills, etc.
- Develop and implement reference-checking policies; create a list of questions.
- Schedule a brief training session for all staff members to teach skills for reviewing applications and welcoming interview candidates.
- Develop a format for second and third interviews.
- Develop a "Mystery Applicant" program and announce it to all managers.

Managing for Retention Strategy

- Develop and implement new-employee orientation plan; assign key staff members as "shepherds."

- Implement monthly staff training program and pre-shift meetings for each department.

- Develop regular performance evaluation policies, formats and schedules for all staff members.

- Develop an exit interview format and a list of standard exit interview questions.

- Implement a sales training program for front-of-the-house staff.

- Create incentive, contest and reward guidelines for all departments in your operation.

- Identify management tasks that could be delegated to employees; contact colleges to set up internships for employee workers who take on management tasks that apply to their majors.

- Schedule a "Managing for Retention" training session for all managers. Discuss and fine-tune your operation's policies and procedures, staff incentives, etc.; create an employee handbook; discuss your operation's expectations for effective staff leadership and communication.

"Take care of your employees and the guest will follow."

—David Precopia, Vice President, Black-eyed Pea International

One More Way To Turn the Tables on Turnover...

The Service That Sells! Success Profile Employee Selection Tool

With the *Service That Sells! Success Profile* — an employee selection tool designed specifically for each position in your restaurant or even customized for your own operation — you can systematically match the right person with the right job and save time in the process by interviewing only the applicants who fit the job in any industry (quick-service, full-service, family service) and any position (management as well as front and back of the house).

Off-the-shelf product is just $239 for six months of unlimited use. (SP-101). Call 1-800-247-8514 for information on custom applications that are available to meet a chain operation's specific needs. (Custom applications can be delivered in the format that works best for you — disk, point-of-sale touch-screen, terminal, or paper and pencil.)

More Books in the 52 Ways Series

Pump Up Your Profits: 52 Ways to Build Your Bottom Line book

Packed with 52 hot tips and cold, hard statistics, this book will save you *thousands* in one year (a total of $354,771.08 if every idea applied to your restaurant). Check it out and find out an idea a day to save your operation cash! (PUB-541) $19.95.

All for One: 52 Ways to Build a Winning Team book

Written just for restaurants, this book reveals why teams thrive or die, how to choose the right team players, develop strategic team plays that unite all of the staff, coach members to use their individual skills for the benefit of the team, motivate the team to outperform the competition and show your staff when the team wins, they win! (PUB-543) $19.95.

Playing Games at Work: 52 Best Incentives, Contests & Rewards book

Improve sales, service and safety, build teamwork, increase product knowledge and reduce waste-watching — all with this book that motivates employees with some of the best incentives, contests and rewards! (PUB-520) $19.95.

Pour It On: 52 Ways to Maximize Bar Sales book

Determine the right price for all your beverage items, out-*present* the competition, instead of out-*pricing* them, create fun marketing promotions that keep your guests coming back and teach your staff wine and hand-crafted beer basics. (PUB-540) $19.95.

The Foundation of Pencom: *Service That Sells!* Products

Service That Sells! The Art of Profitable Hospitality book

This is it. The best-selling book in foodservice history! Over the years we've updated it and, based on demand, kept printing it. Today, hundreds of thousands of copies later, owners, managers and operators are still using it for its "1001 ways to make your restaurant more profitable." English (PUB-513) and Spanish (PUB-513S) editions $16.95. French (PUB-513F) $24.95.

Quick *Service That Sells!* book

Learn the secrets to quick service success with this book that reveals: how national marketing campaigns can hurt you; the seven words that can make you thousands; why just saying

"I'm sorry" doesn't work with handling guests complaints; hidden places to find new (and great!) employees and much more! (PUB-512) $16.95.

Service That Sells! Video

Our book was so successful, we brought it to life and created this award-winning video. It demonstrates the *Service That Sells!* concepts in action and shows your entire staff how they can make more money — and how you can, too! Two versions, full service (alcohol sales) and family (no alcohol sales). Full-service (TVC-25), Family (TVC-31) $99.

Service That Sells! Video Workbooks

How do you remember what you learn? You practice it every day. Interactive staff workbooks increase retention and ensure top performances — for as little as $2 per person. (TW-26) 25 for $69.95, 50 for $99.95.

Service That Sells! Newsletter

News you can use. Every month, you'll learn new ways to increase sales and decrease costs — and, as a subscriber, you'll receive free posters and a 10 percent year-end rebate to use on any Pencom products. Just $99 for a year U.S. subscription. (NL-101). Call for international rates.

Quick *Service That Sells!* Newsletter

The only monthly newsletter written exclusively for quick-service restaurants. Packed with ideas guaranteed to make your operation run smoother. Just $79 for a one-year subscription, $129 for two years. Multiple subscription rates available. Canadian subscriptions are $119. Other international subscriptions are $149. (NL-102)

More Sales And Service Products From Pencom

Slam Dunk Marketing book

If people learn best through parables, and you know they do, then you're sure to soak up skills in this fictional (but true to life!) best-selling story of a restaurant owner. As you follow Dean's experiences, you'll learn how to market your restaurant on a shoestring budget, personalize your direct mail, calculate your *real* return on investment, train your staff how to execute your marketing campaigns and accurately determine if your plan will work *before* you execute it. (PUB-544) $16.95.

Pour On the Profits video

With this video, you'll dramatically increase your bar sales and improve your service with innovative strategies like table talk (break down the barrier between the server and the guest), product knowledge vs. product wisdom (educate your staff about the bar products and teach how to excite their guests with what they know) and sales behavior and upselling. (TVC-61) $99.

CheckBusters: The Art of Smart Selling video program

A fast-paced video and interactive workbooks create a fun program that raises your check averages by a *minimum* of 25 cents per person — or your money back! Ideal for servers, bartenders, greeters and managers. Video (TVC-26) $149; workbooks (TW-26), 25 for $69.95, 50 for $99.95.

Show Time video program

Every time a server steps up to a table, the spotlight's on. How well each server performs determines how well you profit. This program, a 15-minute, high-powered video and accompanying workbooks, uses a step-by-step approach to show your staff how to perform *and* profit. Video (TVC-53) $99, workbooks (TW-53), 25 for $39.95, 50 for $49.95.

Curtain Time for managers video
After your staff has studied *Show Time*, this 15-minute training implementation video, shows managers how to reinforce what they learned using role-playing scenarios. Improve service, build morale and create an all-star cast. (TVC-54) $69.

Work Smarter, Not Harder
These skillbooks with real-world restaurant scenarios teach your servers and bartenders 21 strategies guaranteed to raise guest checks 25 cents per person! Choose from full-service (PUB-519) and family-dining (PUB-522) versions. Pricing starts at $8.95*.

* Minimum order of 10 required. Call 1-800-247-8514 for information on bulk discounts.

Seminars, Consulting and Management Tools

Seminars/On-Site Training
Pencom International offers a full range of results-oriented seminars — from sales and service to internal marketing strategies and leadership skills. Call 1-800-247-8514 for more information.

Restaurant Consulting
From start up to crisis management, Pencom International helps you find solutions to your biggest challenges with our complete, confidential and detailed restaurant consulting services that can be provided via telephone or a personal visit to your operation. Call 1-800-247-8514 for more information.

"All I Said Was..." Sexual Harassment video

Have you been meaning to implement sexual harassment training BUT:

- You just haven't gotten around to it?
- You don't think you have a problem at your operation?
- You're worried that if you "educate" your employees, you'll help them figure out how to sue you?
- It takes too much time and money to take people away from their jobs for this kind of training?

If you answered "yes" to any of these questions, this video program is for you! Designed by employment lawyers who want to help businesses fight back against the increasing trend of lawsuits, this program (two less-than-30-minute videos) can help protect your company from the devastating costs of a sexual harassment action. Your investment in this program and requirement that every employee and manager watch one of the videos will be powerful evidence in your defense if you're sued, and may help you avoid a lawsuit altogether.

- *"All I Said Was..."* Staff Version — demonstrates to your staff the importance of eliminating sexual content from conversations and consequences from "innocent" remarks (TVC-63) $99

- *"All I Said Was..."* Manager's Version — shows managers how to deal with complaints and implement a sensible policy (TVC-62) $99

Protect your business by ordering both videos today. Special package for both (PKG-1600) $159.

Call **1-800-247-8514** to order these products or for a **free catalog** of other Pencom International training and marketing solutions.

Three easy ways to order using the form on the next page:

Please clip or photocopy and mail to Pencom International, P.O. Box 1920, Denver, CO 80201, fax to 1-800-746-2211 or call 1-800-247-8514 for immediate service.

1. ORDERED BY

Print name	Title
Company name	
Address (Please no P.O. Boxes)	This address is: ❏ Home ❏ Business
City	State	Zip
Telephone # (Required to process order)	Fax #

2. SHIP TO *(IF DIFFERENT)*

Print name	Title
Company name	
Address (Please no P.O. Boxes) ❏ Home ❏ Business	
City	State	Zip
Telephone # (Required)	Fax #

3. METHOD OF PAYMENT

❏ I've enclosed check # _____ payable to Pencom

❏ Please charge to the following credit card:

❏ American Express *(15 digits)*   ❏ Discover *(16 digits)*

❏ MasterCard *(16 digits)*   ❏ Visa *(13 or 16 digits)*

1	2	3	4	5	6	7	8	9	10	11	12	13	14	15	16

Expiration Date

Print Cardholder's Name

4. ORDER

Product Code	Title	Quantity	Unit Price	Total

5. SHIPPING AND HANDLING

Continental U.S.	Merchandise total
❏ **Standard Two-Day Delivery via Airborne Express**	
All orders for in-stock items are shipped within 24 hours after we receive your order. Most orders will be delivered within 2 days of shipment. Add $4.95 for the first item and $1.75 for each additional item.	Shipping & handling *(see left)*
❏ **Guaranteed Next Business Day Delivery via Airborne Express**	Subtotal
Orders for in-stock items received by noon MST will be shipped that day and delivered the next day. Orders received after 12 noon will be shipped the next day and delivered within 24 hours of shipment. Add $9.95 for the first item and $1.75 for each additional item.	Colorado residents *(add 7.3% sales tax)*
Call For Rates Outside the Continental U.S.	Grand total